Stitch A Child's Quilt

Vicki M. A. Thomas

American Quilter's Society

P. O. Box 3290 • Paducah, KY 42002-3290

Located in Paducah, Kentucky, the American Quilter's Society (AQS) is dedicated to promoting the accomplishments of today's quilters. Through its publications and events, AQS strives to honor today's quiltmakers and their work and to inspire future creativity and innovation in quiltmaking.

EDITOR: BARBARA SMITH
BOOK DESIGN/ILLUSTRATIONS: CASSIE A. ENGLISH
PATTERN ILLUSTRATIONS: ANGELA SCHADE
COVER DESIGN: MICHAEL BUCKINGHAM
PHOTOGRAPHY: CHARLES R. LYNCH

Library of Congress Cataloging-in-Publication Data
Thomas, Vicki M. A.
    Stitch a child's quilt / Vicki M. A. Thomas.
                    p.   cm.
    ISBN 1-57432-721-6
    1. Patchwork Patterns. 2. Quilting Patterns. 3. Children's quilts. I. Title.
TT835.T4638   1999
746.46'041--dc21   99-14909
                                         CIP

Additional copies of this book may be ordered from the American Quilter's Society, PO Box 3290, Paducah, KY 42002-3290 @ $19.95. Add $2.00 for postage and handling.

Acknowledgments

Some of my friends and my husband have contributed countless hours of personal time and talent toward the construction and completion of this book and the quilts in it. I would like to give a heart-felt "thank you" to each of them. They have been more than generous and have given me a tremendous gift. I sincerely appreciate their efforts, because this book would not have been possible without them. I also owe my two youngest children a great deal of thanks and hugs for being so patient (sometimes), and putting up with the lack of personal attention and play time while Mom and Dad spent so much time working on this book.

Hand Quilting
Alecia Knox
Leesa Lloyd
Ginger Obst

Pattern and Instruction Testing
Ethel Bill

Donation of Materials
Cindy Schwiesow
Ginger Obst

Instructional Diagrams and Illustrations
My wonderful husband, Patrick Thomas

I also want to extend a special thank you to the American Quilter's Society for giving me the opportunity of a lifetime – the publishing of my first book of quilt patterns.

CONTENTS

The symbols by each quilt project will help you evaluate whether the pattern is the right skill level for you.

 = easy if you have some sewing experience.

 = you may want to practice new techniques.

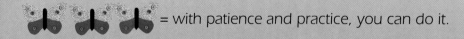 = with patience and practice, you can do it.

ABOUT THIS BOOK

All the patterns in this book are my own creations. Most came from observing the things that children find fascinating. Others were created because of the lack of available patterns for the subject I wanted, and still others were designed because of something I saw that provoked an idea or struck me as pleasing.

I have tried to produce a book that sparks the interest of others and encourages quilting as adventuresome and satisfying. The focus is to provide instruction for using the patterns in this book. It is not intended to teach sewing or quilting. From personal experience, I recommend to anyone interested in quilting that you join a local quilt guild. These organizations provide a wealth of knowledge and encouragement. You will be challenged and inspired by everything you learn and by the sheer talent of others. I learned more from my guild members in the last few years than I learned in 10 years on my own. It is a wonderful, friendly environment in which to learn all the things you need to know and to try new things.

The quilt projects are marked with symbols showing the suggested skill level. If you are a beginning quilter, you may want to start with the patterns marked "easy" and work your way up to the patterns that require more skill. The skills needed to reproduce these quilts are explained in Cutting and Piecing Techniques (page 8). They are suggested reading for anyone using these patterns and are referred to many times.

The fabric requirements stated for each quilt have been adjusted slightly to allow a little extra, but you may want to add a quarter yard to each fabric to allow you to make samples of the less familiar techniques.

The binding yardage listed is optional. Many of the quilts have been finished with the quick-turn method, in which the layers are sewn around the edges. The quilt is turned right side out through an unsewn portion of the seam (page 15).

The quilt sizes can be made larger or smaller by simply increasing or decreasing the number of blocks. My suggestion is, when changing a quilt size, draw the new size on graph paper so you will have a visual reference of the new setting. When increasing the size, remember to buy extra yardage, which you can figure on a percentage basis. For instance, if the quilt pattern has 20 blocks and you want to add another row of four blocks, you will need to buy at least 20 percent more fabric (4 divided by 20 = 20%).

I pieced all the quilt tops in this book by machine. Most of the quilts have been machine quilted or have a combination of machine and hand quilting. You can quilt your project any way you like, but the beginning hand quilter might enjoy using a ¼"-wide masking tape made especially for quilting. The tapes are marked 9 or 12 stitches to the inch, showing you where to place every stitch. The tapes will help you make evenly spaced stitches. They can be found in quilt stores or ordered from quilting-supply catalogs.

For children's quilts, don't be afraid to use bright colors, loud patterns, and fun prints. Children love them. And, if I've learned anything from my mother, it's this: some colors and patterns may not seem that good stacked together, but they can be wonderful in a finished design. I don't know how many times I've told my mother that her selections seemed strange to me, but I have been awestruck by the completed piece. Her choice and placement of color are amazing. I may never know the secret to her imagination for color and pattern, but I keep trying, and I hope you will, too. It's all a matter of personal taste.

TOOLS AND SUPPLIES

Following is a list of the basic and most frequently used equipment in quilt making.

BATTING

The batting is what gives a quilt its thickness and warmth. There are several types on the market. The type used in most quilts is a low-loft, cotton-polyester blend, which makes the quilt fairly thin and flat. This batting is preferred for hand quilting. A higher loft will produce a puffier quilt, more like that of a comforter. If using polyester batting, get the bonded type for uniform thickness and stability. You will want to read the manufacturer's information and instructions.

These are the standard sizes for available batting:

Crib	45" x 60"
Twin	72" x 90"
Full/Double	81" x 96"
Queen	90" x 108"
King	120" x 120"

ROTARY CUTTER

The rotary cutter has a round blade mounted at the end of a handle with a safety cover for the blade. Extreme care must be taken when using this tool because it is very sharp. Make it a habit to always close the safety cover after every cut. The cutter comes in three sizes: small, medium, and large. The medium-size cutter is best for the efficiency and control needed for most quilting projects. The smaller cutter can be used for curved designs, and the large cutter is good for cutting several layers at a time.

RULERS

The rulers needed for rotary cutting should be made of thick, clear, acrylic plastic. There are several shapes available: rectangles, squares, triangles, and bias angles, to name just a few.

A most useful and most practical one is the 6" x 24" ruler. It is marked in ⅛" increments and has 45-degree angle markings.

CUTTING MAT

A self-healing cutting mat is needed for use with a rotary cutter. It is marked with a 1" grid and 45-degree angles to help in lining up fabric for cutting. An 18" x 24" size, or larger, is recommended.

EVEN-FEED (WALKING) FOOT

This attachment to the sewing machine is a special presser foot that feeds the top and bottom layers through the machine at the same rate of speed, so the bottom layer doesn't get ahead of the top one. This foot is recommended for machine quilting and attaching binding.

FABRIC

The recommended fabric is a high-quality, 100-percent cotton. Fabrics that are stretchy, very thick, too stiff, or loosely woven are difficult to use and should probably be avoided. Generally speaking, the fabrics should be washed, dried, and ironed before using, especially if you intend to hand stitch a quilt.

Washing a fabric removes chemicals and excess dyes and will preshrink the fabric. Washing also allows you to test for colorfastness. A fabric that continues to bleed its color after several rinses should not be used. Some people prefer not to prewash their fabrics because the sizing in the unwashed fabric makes the pieces easier to handle for machine sewing. When quilts made with unwashed fabrics are washed, they may shrink and acquire a puckered antique look, which some people prefer. The choice is up to you.

IRON AND IRONING BOARD

Use an iron that has a steam setting. Be sure to place your ironing board at a comfortable height and close to the sewing area, because it will be used frequently.

MARKERS

These are used to mark quilting patterns on fabric. A water-soluble pen or pencil is a good choice because no permanent marks will be left on the finished quilt. It's a good idea to test your markers on your fabrics to be sure they will wash out.

MASKING TAPE

Masking tape can be used to temporarily mark some quilting patterns and as a guide for top stitching. The tape comes in a ¼"-wide roll. It is perfect for marking ¼" echo quilting lines around block patterns, and it leaves no permanent mark. The tape can also be used as a ¼" seam allowance guide for sewing.

PINS

The long, thin, sharp quilting pins are most often recommended. Dressmaker pins will do fine, however. Whatever type you use, be sure they are sharp and rust-proof.

SAFETY PINS

These can be used to pin baste the quilt for machine quilting. The recommended size is 1", and you will want to buy rust-proof, nickel-plated pins. Approximately 300 are enough for a small quilt, and 500 or more may be needed for a large quilt.

SCISSORS

Shears are generally used to cut fabric and pattern pieces. They are also needed for trimming bat-ting and excess fabric or cutting curved pieces.

SMALL THREAD SCISSORS OR SNIPS

Small scissors, the size of embroidery scissors, or snips, are great for cutting threads as you remove work from the machine or for clipping stray threads from the finished quilt.

SEAM RIPPER

This tool is for removing unwanted stitches. Even highly experienced quilters need to use it occasionally.

SEWING MACHINE AND ACCESSORIES

The sewing machine is an obvious tool for quilt making unless you intend to do all the piecing and quilting by hand. Most of us don't have the time required for hand work, so we rely on the machine. The type of machine is not important as long as it is capable of sewing for long periods of time without overheating.

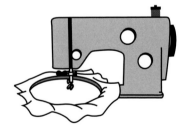

It should have the capability of doing the simple straight stitch at about 11 stitches per inch. A throat plate with only a small needle hole is recommended. A presser foot that accurately measures a ¼" seam allowance is also recommended but not necessary. There are other ways to keep the measurement correct.

Keep a sharp needle in the machine and use the size, recommended by your manufacturer for cottons. The type of thread most often used is a 100-percent cotton or a cotton-wrapped polyester.

QUILTING HOOPS AND FRAMES

If you intend to hand quilt, you will probably want a quilting hoop or a frame. These are needed to hold the layers of a quilt taut for hand quilting. Quilting hoops, similar to embroidery hoops only larger, come in various sizes. Choose the one most comfortable for you to hold.

QUILTING NEEDLES

Called "betweens," these hand-quilting needles range in size from 7 to 13. The larger the number, the finer and smaller the needle size. "Sharps" are longer and have larger eyes. They are generally used for hand piecing.

QUILTING THREAD

Used for hand quilting, this is heavier than regular thread and is coated to help it slide through the fabric more easily and prevent tangles.

THIMBLE

This tool is used for hand sewing to prevent hurting the finger that pushes the needle through the fabric and to give extra push when working with several layers of fabrics. There are several types available. Use the most comfortable one for you.

Cutting and Piecing Techniques

The following techniques were used to create the quilts in this book. To some, this information may provide a useful review, but beginning quilters may want to read through this section carefully before beginning their projects.

Fabrics

The yardage requirements for the patterns are based on 44"–45" wide fabrics. The best fabric to use for quilting is 100-percent cotton. No matter what fabrics you use, try to buy the best material you can afford so your quilts will last longer.

Cutting

It is highly recommended that, as patches are cut, they be labeled. The easiest way to do this is to write the patch letter or description, and any other information you need, on a small piece of paper and pin it to a stack of like patches. For quilts with many pieces, it's best to place the patches in labeled plastic zippered bags to keep them organized and to guard against loss.

Before cutting out all your fabric patches, you may want to sew a test block to ensure that the templates and pattern pieces have been cut correctly. A sample block will also give you an opportunity to test your color selections. If you don't like a particular fabric, you can change it without wasting more time and fabric.

When you are happy with your choices, cut the rest of the patches. To cut several like patches at one time, you can layer the fabrics. It's best to use no more than four layers at a time to keep them from slipping while you cut.

There are two ways to cut patches: using templates and rotary cutting.

Templates are copies of pattern pieces made of plastic, lightweight cardboard, or heavy paper. The easiest way to make a template is to trace each pattern piece from the book onto quilter's template plastic with a permanent marker. Be sure to use a ruler to trace the straight lines. Cut out the templates with sharp scissors. Accuracy is important because any irregularities in the template will be transferred to every patch made with that template. To use a template, place it face down on the wrong side of your fabric and trace the template with a fabric marker or quilter's pencil. You can put a sheet of fine-grain sandpaper under the fabric to keep it from shifting while you trace.

Template labels followed by "r" (for example, Ar) denote using the pattern piece in reverse (mirror image). Simply turn the template over to draw the reverse or place two pieces of fabric together, with right sides facing, to cut both the pattern piece and its reverse at the same time.

Cut the fabric pieces with sharp scissors. Straight lines can be cut with a rotary cutter and ruler, if you like. To cut several patches at one time, you can layer the fabrics. To cut with scissors, put a pin in the center of the pattern area through all the layers to keep them from shifting while you cut. You will not need to pin the layers for rotary cutting.

Full-size patch patterns in this book include ¼" seam allowances. The dashed line indicates the seam line. Machine piecers usually cut out templates on the solid line. For hand piecers, and some machine piecers, who want to have a drawn sewing line on their patches, cut out templates on the dashed line. Then trace the templates on your fabric, leaving room between patches (at least ½") to add seam allowances by eye as you cut.

Full-size block section patterns, such as those presented for the variations in the patterns Up, Up, and Away (page 85) and I Believe in Angels (page 92), do not have seam allowances. To make a template from this type of pattern, trace each piece individually, then if needed, draw ¼" seam allowances around the tracing with a see-through ruler.

Rotary cutting provides an alternative to making templates, but not all patches can be easily rotary cut. For example, some of the patches in Patchwork Planes (page 25) are measured in sixteenths, and many rulers do not show sixteenths. Therefore, no rotary cutting instructions are given for these patches.

Rotary cutting is useful for simple geometric shapes, such as squares, rectangles, and triangles that have dimensions easily measured with a ruler. For these patches, measurements are given on the pattern pieces. Look for the little rotary cutter symbol. Use the first measurement as the strip width. Cut strips as needed across the fabric from selvage to selvage. Use the second measurement for cutting patches from the strips. Please note that the rotary cutting measurements include seam allowances.

Half-square triangles. Here is an easy way to create accurate triangles without using templates. Using the rotary measurements given in your chosen pattern, cut squares from strips. Then cut the squares in half diagonally to make the triangles. The triangles will contain ¼" seam allowances. This method yields two triangles per square, in which the fabric grain runs parallel to the short sides of the triangles.

Quarter-square triangles. Squares can also be cut on both diagonals to yield four triangles per square, with the fabric grain running parallel to the long sides of the triangles.

BLOCK ASSEMBLY

Quilt blocks are assembled in units: small units are sewn together to make larger units, and these units are joined to make even larger units, and so on.

QUICK PIECING

There are some piecing short cuts that are fun and easy to do. Wherever a quick-piecing method can be used instead of cutting individual patches, it is indicated in the patterns along with the measurement for cutting, using that particular method.

Strip piecing is a quick-piecing method in which several strips of fabric are sewn together lengthwise to form a band. The bands can be used as sashing or borders, or they

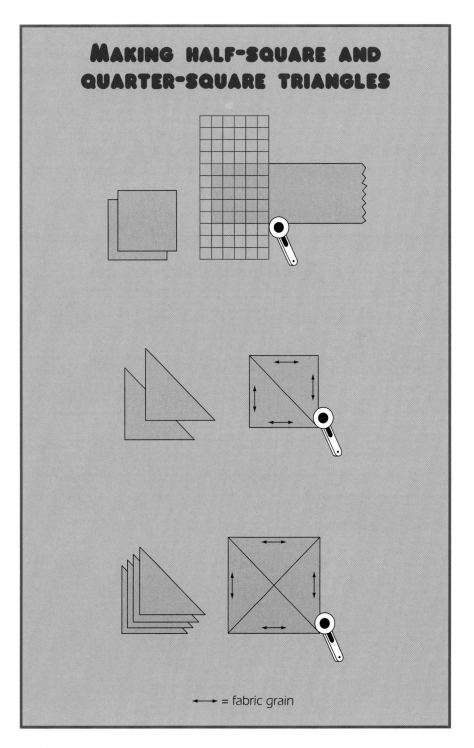

MAKING HALF-SQUARE AND QUARTER-SQUARE TRIANGLES

◄──► = fabric grain

can be sliced to create units. When strip-pieced units are sewn together, a complete block can be made quickly and easily.

Chain piecing is the process of sewing patches or units together, one after the other, without lifting the presser foot or cutting the threads in between. After several units have been sewn in this way, they can be pressed and cut apart. With this method, you can sew all the like seams in all the blocks in your quilt at one time. Then, when the last seam has been sewn, all the blocks will be complete.

Add-a-strip piecing, which is useful for patterns like the Log Cabin, is similar to chain piecing. For this method, patches or units are sewn, one after another, to a long strip. The most accurate way to do this is to leave a small space between the pieces as you sew. Then, with a rotary cutter and ruler, make two cuts to separate the pieces.

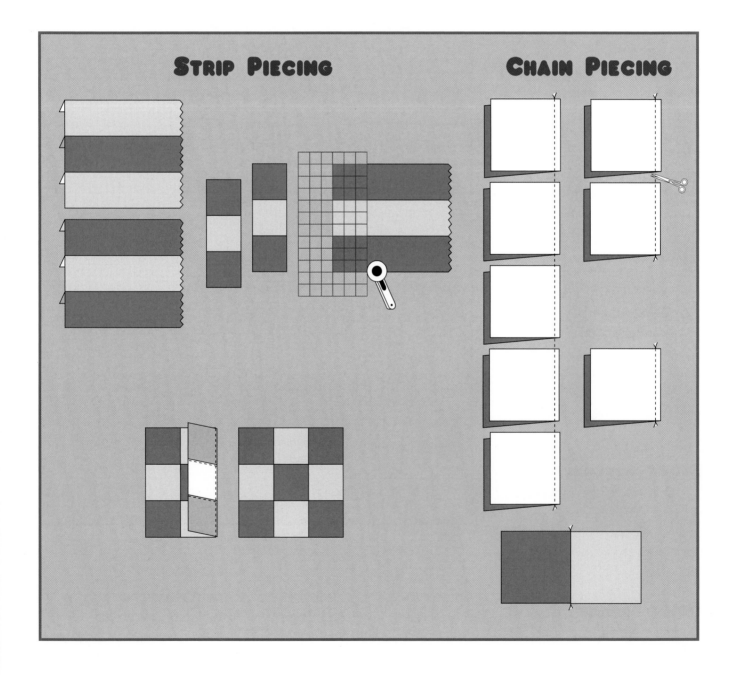

Quick corner is a technique for replacing the corners of a square or rectangle with triangles. Please note that half-square triangles are too large to use for cutting quick corners.

For the quick corner technique, use a ruler and a pencil to draw a sewing line on the back of a square, from one corner to the opposite corner.

Align the square with one corner of a square or larger rectangle, right sides facing, and sew the two pieces together on the drawn line.

To check the accuracy of the seam, fold the square back on itself at the stitching line. If the two unsewn corners of the square meet, then the piece is sewn correctly. If the corners do not meet, remove the stitches and resew. When the piece has been sewn correctly, trim off the excess fabric, leaving a ¼" seam allowance.

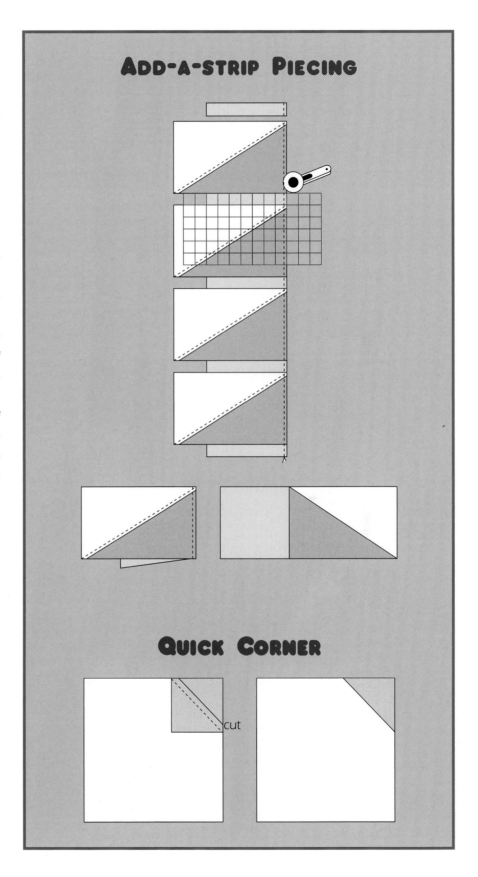

ADD-A-STRIP PIECING

QUICK CORNER

cut

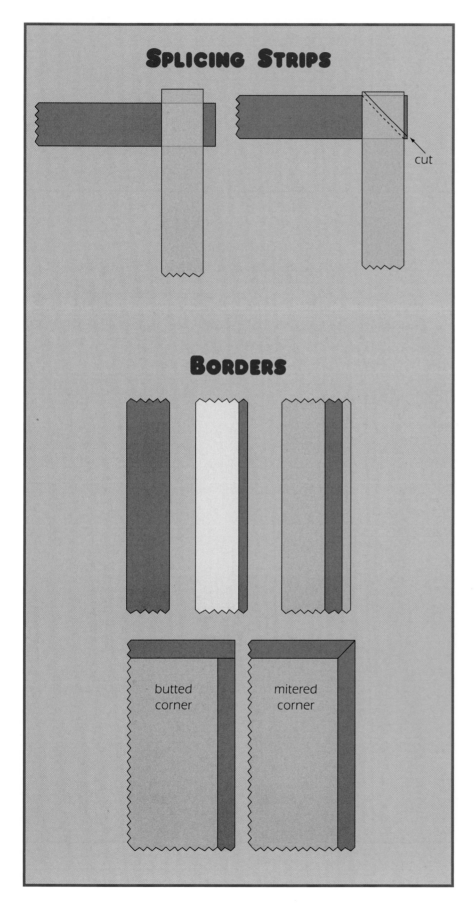

SPLICING STRIPS

cut

BORDERS

butted corner

mitered corner

SPLICING STRIPS

Most sashing and border strips can be cut across the fabric from selvage to selvage, but sometimes, strips are required that are longer than the fabric is wide. When this is the case, you can sew strips together to create the length needed. An attractive seam can be made by sewing the strips at a 45-degree angle. The easiest way to do this is to lay one strip on top of the other, right sides together, as shown in the figure. With a pencil and a ruler, mark a line from "corner" to "corner." Sew along the drawn line, then cut off the excess fabric, leaving a ¼" seam allowance. Press the seam allowances open to distribute bulk.

BORDERS

Borders frame the quilt-top design and accent your work. The style used is strictly a matter of personal preference. The simplest border is just a width of fabric in a print or solid. The width can vary depending on the desired look. A multiple border can be made by sewing strips of varying widths together.

The method of joining borders at the corners can be an important part of a quilt's design. The two most common treatments are the butted and the mitered corner.

The borders in the patterns are cut extra long to allow a margin for error. To attach a border to the quilt top, mark the center of each edge of the quilt and the center of each border strip on its long edge. Match the centers when pinning border strips to your quilt.

For butted corners, sew the border strips to the long sides of the quilt top by using the following method: Pin a strip along one edge, right sides together. The strip should extend beyond the quilt top, at both ends, by about 1". Sew the borders to the top with a ¼" seam allowance. Press the borders away from the quilt top and trim the ends even with the quilt's edges. Attach the border strips to the short sides in the same manner.

For Mitered corners, pin a border strip to one side of the quilt, right sides together. At the corners, the strip should extend past the quilt edges by the width of the border plus about 1". Start sewing the strip ¼" in from the corner of the quilt top and use a backstitch to anchor the sewing line. Sew the full length of the strip, stopping ¼" before the next corner and backstitch again. This ¼" is important because all three seams, that is, the two border seams and the mitered corner seam, must all meet at the same spot. Attach the other three border strips in the same manner, being careful to start and end the seams ¼" from the corners.

To complete the miter, fold the quilt top in half diagonally, right sides together. Align the borders' seam lines and raw edges. Push the seam allowances toward the quilt top, so you can see the seam intersections at the corner.

Align the 45-degree line of a ruler with the raw edges of the borders. Slide the ruler along the borders to the right until it touches the

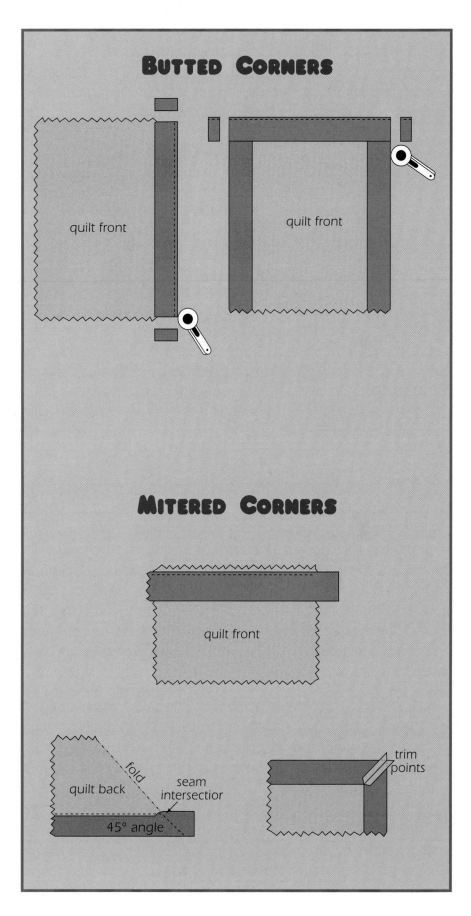

spot where the three seams meet. (Don't try to make the ruler align with the fold.) Check to make sure that the 45-degree line is still aligned with the raw edges. Mark the border strip along the ruler to create the stitching line for the miter. Pin the borders together to keep them from shifting as you sew. Be sure to backstitch at the corner to anchor the sewing line, then stitch on the marked line from the seam intersection to the border edge.

Trim off the excess fabric, leaving a ¼" seam allowance. Open the fold and press the seam allowances to one side. Sew the other corners in the same manner.

PRESSING

Using a good steam iron, press seams as pieces are sewn. Do not slide the iron back and forth across the surface of the pieces. Instead, press straight down, then pick the iron up to move it to another area, or glide the iron very gently across small areas. Sliding the iron or pushing too hard can stretch the fabric, resulting in uneven triangles and lopsided squares, both of which can cause difficulties during assembly. If a piece has been stretched out of shape, it would be best to cut a replacement.

Press seam allowances toward the darkest fabric whenever possible to keep them from showing on the front of the finished quilt. Pressing all pieces and seams throughout the construction of the blocks and the quilt top will help make a smooth finished quilt that lies flat. Pressing

also helps to show where bulging and mismatched seams are and whether the work is square or crooked, giving you an opportunity to fix small problems before they become bigger ones.

LAYERING

Before layering your quilt top with batting and backing, first check to be sure that the top lies flat. There should be no puckers, waves, stretched areas, or unsewn seams. If there are problems, now is the time to fix them. On the back of the quilt, trim off loose sewing threads and frayed edges.

The day before you want to layer your quilt, it's best if you can take the batting out of the package and lay it flat. Press the quilt top to remove any wrinkles and iron the material that will be used for the backing. Flannel makes a good backing for baby quilts because it is soft and warm. Be sure to prewash flannel because it tends to shrink quite a bit.

The batting and backing should be cut 4" to 6" wider and longer than the quilt top. If the backing needs to be pieced, sew the panels together and press the seam allowances open.

If you intend to use the quick-turn technique to finish the edges of your quilt, skip to Quick-Turn Finishing on the next page. If you want to bind the edges of your quilt, use the following directions:

To layer a quilt for binding, center the backing, right side down, on a table. If it's a good table, protect

the surface with something that will keep it from being scratched, such as oilcloth. The quilt layers can hang over the table edges. Center the batting on the backing, then center the quilt top on the batting, right side up.

If you have a helper, you can stand on opposite sides of the table, reach under the quilt top and batting and pull simultaneously on the backing to make it taut. Go all around the table, pulling on the backing. Do not pull on the batting. Smooth the batting and quilt top gently. If you do not have someone to help you, you can pull against a hand placed in the middle of the quilt. Move your hand along the mid-line of the quilt as you move around the table and pull on the backing.

You will want to baste the layers about every 4" with needle and thread or nickel-plated safety pins. If you use thread, your stitches can be as long as the needle will allow. Baste in a grid, starting along the mid-line and working outward. When the section on the table has been basted, move another section of the quilt onto the table. Pull the backing and smooth the batting and quilt top as before and continue basting. After the whole quilt has been basted, trim the extra batting and batting to about 2" from the quilt top all around. Fold this extra batting and backing over the raw quilt edges to protect them and baste or pin in place. Quilt as desired, then skip to Continuous Binding on the next page.

QUICK-TURN FINISHING

This section gives instructions for finishing your quilt without applying binding. It is called the "inside-out" or "quick-turn" method. Most of the quilts in this book have been finished this way.

After preparing and pressing the quilt top and backing, you can mark your quilting design, if you like. It's a good idea to test any markers on some scraps from your quilt to make sure the lines will wash out.

Lay the backing on a large table or on the floor, right side up. Lay the quilt top on the backing with the right side down. Smooth out any wrinkles. Trim the backing to the same size as the top. Pin these two layers together around the edges. Sew around the edges with a ¼" seam allowance. Leave an unsewn area 12" to 18" in the middle of the bottom edge of the quilt.

Place the quilt, front side up, on a table or on the floor and smooth out the wrinkles. Center the batting on the quilt and pin the batting to the quilt around the edges. Trim off the excess batting even with the quilt edges. Sew the batting to both quilt top and backing with a ¼" seam allowance all around the edges. Don't sew across the opening at the bottom of the quilt, however. Just stitch the batting to the quilt top at the opening.

Trim away the extra fabric in the corners. Using the opening at the bottom, reach into the quilt and pull the corners, one at a time, through the opening. Before turning each corner right side out, first fold in the seam allowances, which will help make the corners square. Use a blunt object, such as closed scissors, to carefully push out the corners from the inside. After preparing all the corners, pull the rest of the quilt to the outside. Carefully smooth the layers. Pin baste the layers as you smooth the quilt. You will need about 350 pins for a small quilt and 500 or more for a larger quilt.

To finish the opening, fold both of the seam allowances to the inside along the open area and pin. The opening can be whip-stitched closed, or you can machine top stitch very close to the edge. Top stitch ½" in from the edge all around the quilt. This stitching will hold the batting in place and provide a nice finishing touch. Quilt as desired.

CONTINUOUS BINDING

Complete all your quilting before adding the binding. Then trim the batting and backing even with the quilt top edges.

To make straight-grain continuous binding, look at your pattern's Cutting Instructions to find the length of binding needed. For straight-grain binding, cut strips 2½" wide across the fabric from selvage to selvage. As a general rule, you will need one strip for every yard required. (For bias binding, cut strips at a 45-degree angle.) Sew the strips end to end at a 45-degree angle, which will distribute the bulk of the seam allowances (see Splicing Strips, page 12). Fold the continuous strip in half down its length, wrong sides together, and press.

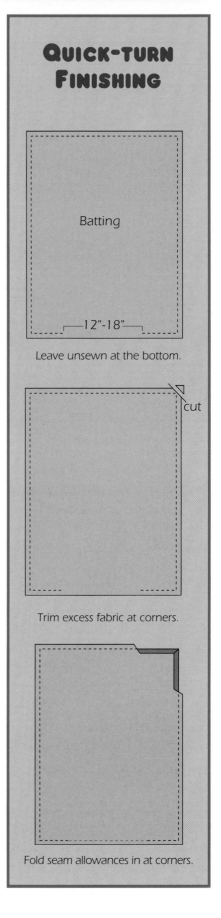

QUICK-TURN FINISHING

Batting

—12"-18"—

Leave unsewn at the bottom.

cut

Trim excess fabric at corners.

Fold seam allowances in at corners.

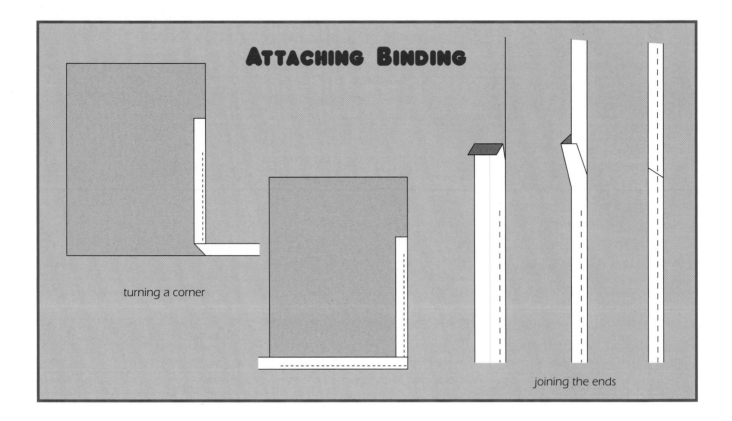

ATTACHING BINDING

turning a corner

joining the ends

Starting somewhere in the middle of a side, not at a corner, align the raw edges of the binding with the raw edge of the quilt top. Leave a tail of at least 3" and start sewing the binding on with a ¼" seam allowance. You may need to use an even-feed (walking) foot to sew the binding on if the layers aren't feeding properly. Stop sewing ¼" from the corner and back stitch to anchor the threads. Cut the threads and remove the quilt from the machine.

To miter a binding corner, fold the strip at a 90-degree angle, as shown in the figure. Then fold the strip aligning the top of the fold with the edge of quilt top. Align the raw edge of the binding strip with the raw edge of the next side of the quilt. Start sewing ¼" in

from the top edge, backstitching to anchor the seam line. Sew to the next corner and miter as before. Continue sewing around the quilt until you are within about 3" of the beginning stitches. Backstitch and remove the quilt from the machine.

Fold under ¼" at the end of one of the strips. Cut off the other end, leave about ½" to tuck into the folded end. Finish sewing the binding. Fold the binding over the raw edges and sew the binding to the back of the quilt by hand with a blind-stitch hem.

A WORD ABOUT QUILTING

The types of quilting stitches in general use are stitch-in-the-ditch, outline (echo) stitch, grids, template designs, and free-hand designs. Alternatively, you can tie the layers togeth-

er with perle cotton, embroidery floss, narrow ribbon, or cotton twine. Most of the projects in this book have been quilted in the ditch, following the designs in the quilt top, but some other quilting ideas have been included for your consideration.

DECORATIONS

These quilts are wonderful for adding all sorts of decorations, and many of the patterns call for buttons, ribbons, bows, and shoelaces. Please be aware that all buttons and other attached decorations are unsuitable for infants and small children because they can present a choking hazard. Even for an older child, it is important to attach buttons and other decorations securely. If anything comes loose during use, repair the quilt immediately.

Patterns

Enough Love To Go Around

This pattern was inspired by a drawing my mother did, a sketch of three rings linked together. I came up with this pattern, adding heart links to express my feelings for my mom. My kids love the way it turned out. Yours will, too. Or, maybe your mom would like one.

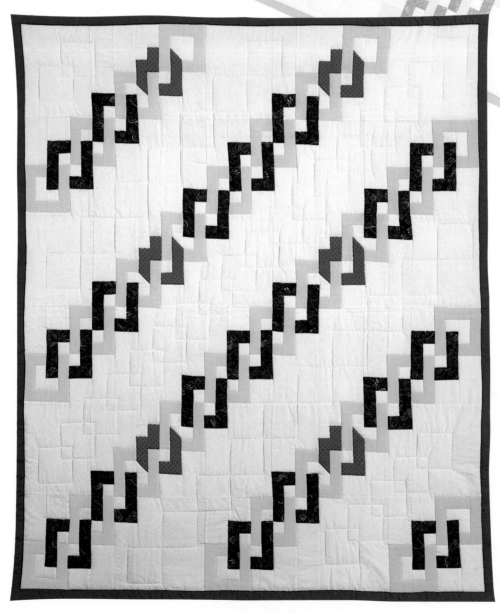

Enough Love to Go Around, hand quilting by Ginger Obst

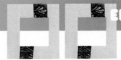

CUTTING INSTRUCTIONS
Quilt 42" x 50"
29 chain blocks, 8" x 8"

Fabrics	Yards	Patches
Yellow (links)	½	40 A, 30 B, 30 C, 30 D
Blue (links)	⅜	20 A, 58 B, 18 C
Red (hearts)	¼	12 A, 18 B, 12 H
Background	1⅞	100 A, 10 B, 30 E, 30F 20 G, 12 H, 6 I, 8 J, 1 K
Border (butted)	⅜	2 strips 1½" x 50½" 2 strips 1½" x 44½"
Backing	3⅛	2 panels 23½" x 54"
Binding (optional)	½	2½" x 5½ yds.
Batting		46" x 54"

CUTTING PATCHES

The Cutting Instructions show the number of patches to cut for each fabric. Cut pieces as they are needed.

SCISSOR CUTTING

Use patterns on page 23-24 to make templates for patches listed under Cutting Instructions. Skip to Piecing Blocks.

ROTARY CUTTING

All of the patches can be rotary cut. The dimensions are given in the patterns, as designated by the rotary cutting symbol. For the H patches, cut 6 red and 6 background squares, 2" x 2". Then cut the squares in half diagonally to make the triangles, which are slightly oversized. After you sew two half-square triangles together, trim the resulting square to 1½" x 1½" (Fig. 1).

PIECING BLOCKS

Make the number of units shown in the Unit Assembly diagrams and use the units to make the blocks (see Block Assembly diagrams). Notice that some units are used upside down.

ASSEMBLING QUILT

Follow the Quilt Assembly diagram for placing the blocks and background piece K. Sew the blocks together in rows across the quilt. Then, sew the rows together.

ADDING BORDERS

Cut five 1½" strips for the borders, selvage to selvage, and splice them as needed to make the lengths given in the Cutting Instructions. Sew the two longest strips to the sides of the quilt top and trim off the extra length even with the edges of the quilt. Add the other two strips to the top and bottom and trim.

FINISHING

Finish the quilt the quick-turn way, then quilt as desired. Or, if you prefer you can quilt the layers and finish the raw edges with binding.

QUILTING IDEAS

1. Quilt in the ditch around all the chain links and along the border seam.
2. Trace the chain seam lines and use the tracing as a quilting pattern in the background areas.
3. Use an over-all design or grid in the background.

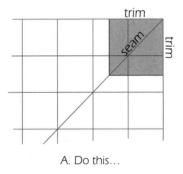

A. Do this…

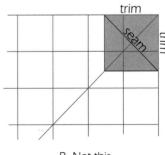

B. Not this

Figure 1. A. Align 45° ruler line with seam to trim half squares. B. Don't align the ruler like this to trim. One triangle will end up smaller than the other.

UNIT ASSEBMLY DIAGRAMS

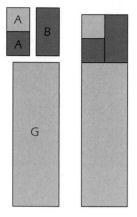

Unit 1–Make 20

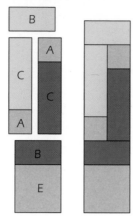

Unit 4–Make 18

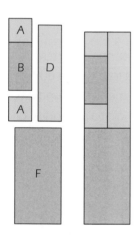

Unit 2–Make 10

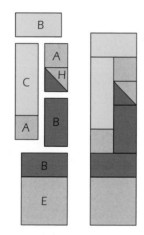

Unit 5–Make 6

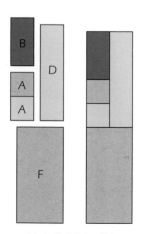

Unit 3–Make 20

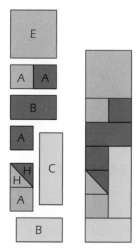

Unit 6–Make 6

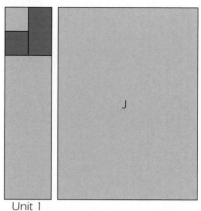

Unit 1

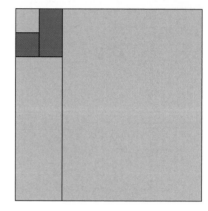

Block 1–Make 8

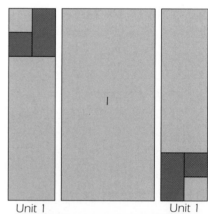

Unit 1   Unit 1

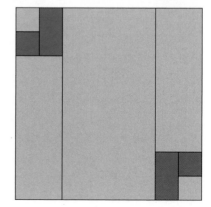

Block 2–Make 6

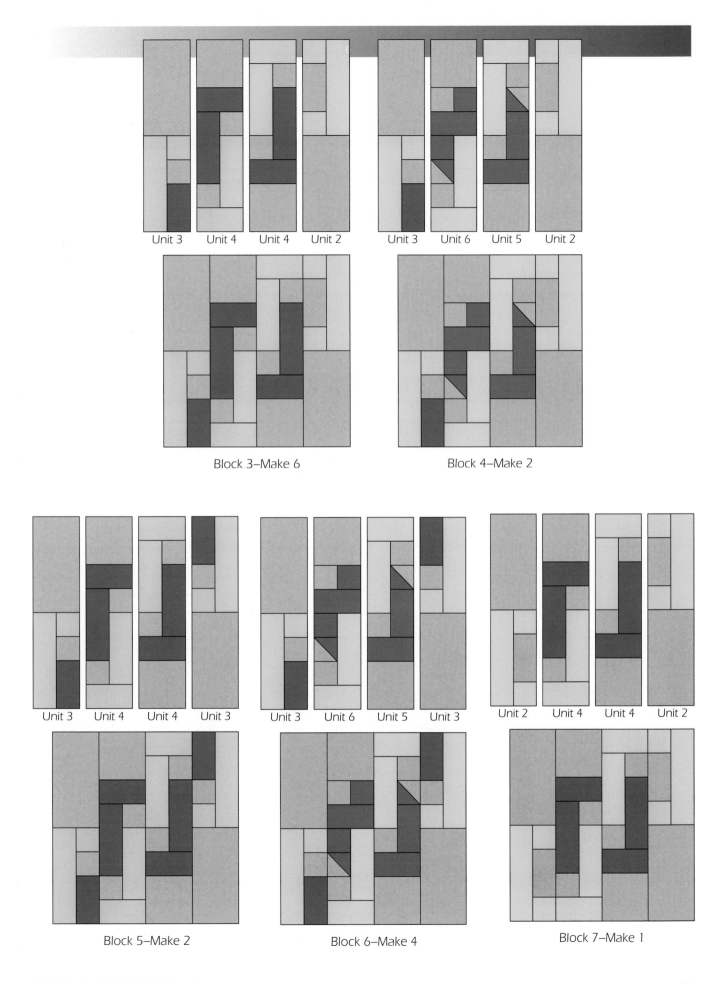

Unit 3 | Unit 4 | Unit 4 | Unit 2 | | Unit 3 | Unit 6 | Unit 5 | Unit 2

Block 3–Make 6   Block 4–Make 2

Unit 3 | Unit 4 | Unit 4 | Unit 3 | | Unit 3 | Unit 6 | Unit 5 | Unit 3 | | Unit 2 | Unit 4 | Unit 4 | Unit 2

Block 5–Make 2   Block 6–Make 4   Block 7–Make 1

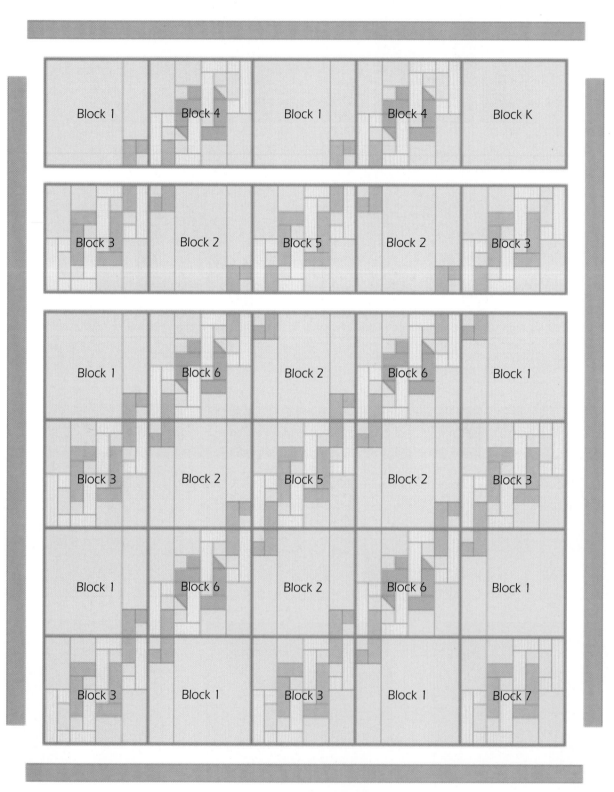

Quilt Assembly. Check to see that blocks are turned correctly before sewing them together.

BACKGROUND ROTARY PIECES

I   8½" x 4½"

J   8½" x 6½"

K   8½" x 8½"
(alternate block)

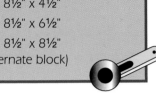

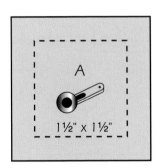

A
1½" x 1½"

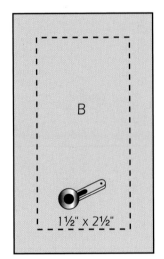

B
1½" x 2½"

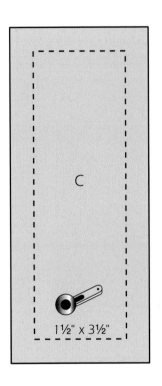

C
1½" x 3½"

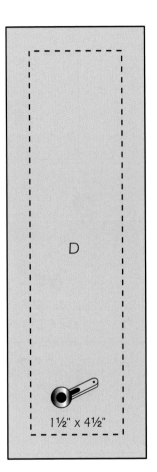

D
1½" x 4½"

Need Help?

Butted corners	p. 13
Chain piecing	p. 10
Quick-turn finishing	p. 15
Rotary cutting	p. 8
Templates	p. 8

E
ENOUGH LOVE
TO GO AROUND

2½" x 2½"

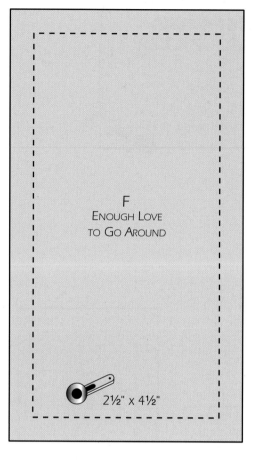

F
ENOUGH LOVE
TO GO AROUND

2½" x 4½"

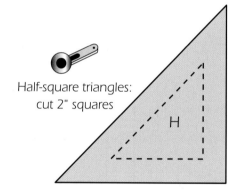

Half-square triangles:
cut 2" squares

H

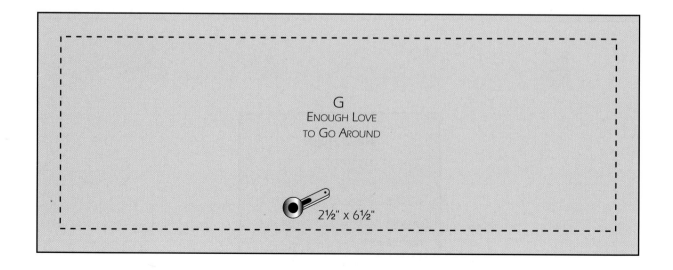

G
ENOUGH LOVE
TO GO AROUND

2½" x 6½"

PATCHWORK PLANES

It's time to take to the skies for a new adventure. This quilt is fun and easy to create, and it will be great for the little pilot in your house.

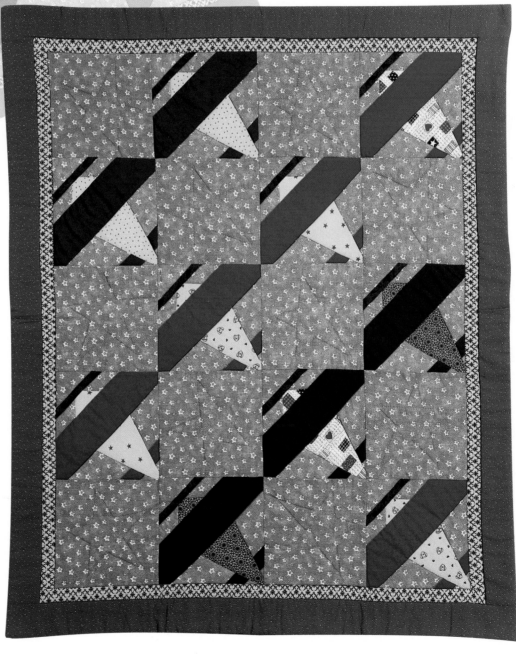

PATCHWORK PLANES, *hand quilting by Ginger Obst*

CUTTING INSTRUCTIONS
Quilt 40" x 48"
10 airplane blocks, 8" x 8"

FABRICS	YARDS	PATCHES
Red 1 (wings/tails)	⅜	5 A, 5 B, 5 Br
Dk. Blue (wings/tails)	⅜	3 A, 3 B, 3 Br
Green (wings/tails)	¼	2 A, 2 B, 2 Br
Red 2 (propellers)	⅛	10 E
5 Light Prints (bodies)	¼ each	2 C & 2 D each
Lt. Blue (background)	1½	10 F, 10 G, 10 Gr 10 H, 10 Hr, 10 I, 10 Ir, 10 J
Inner Border (butted)	¼	2 strips 1½" x 42½" 2 strips 1½" x 36½"
Outer Border (butted)	⅝	2 strips 3½" x 44½" 2 strips 3½" x 42½"
Backing	2⅝	2 panels 27" x 44½"
Binding (optional)	½	2½" x 5¼ yds.
Batting		44" x 52"

CUTTING PATCHES

The Cutting Instructions show the number of patches to cut for each fabric.

SCISSOR CUTTING

Make templates for patches A through J from the patterns on pages 28-30. Cut the number of pieces listed in the Cutting Instructions. Skip to Piecing Blocks.

ROTARY CUTTING

Rotary cutting dimensions are given in the patterns. Look for the rotary cutter symbol. For the F patches, cut five 3⅝" squares from strips. Cut the squares in half diagonally to make the 10 F triangles. Cut 8½" squares for the J pieces. You will need templates for pieces that do not have the rotary cutter symbol.

PIECING BLOCKS

Refer to the Block Assembly and quilt photo for patch placement. Before you begin sewing, arrange the patches for just one block. Stack the other patches for the other blocks on top. Use chain piecing to make all 10 blocks. Don't forget to press the seams as you go.

ASSEMBLING QUILT

Arrange the blocks on the floor, a table, or a bed, alternating them in checkerboard fashion with the solid background squares (J pieces in Quilt Assembly diagram). First, sew the blocks and squares together in rows across the quilt. Then sew the rows together.

ADDING BORDERS

To attach the inner border, sew the 1½" x 42½" strips to the two longest sides first. Trim the strips even with the quilt's edges. Next, attach the 1½" x 36½" strips to the top and bottom of the quilt and trim as before. Press after applying each border piece. Attach the outside border in the same way.

FINISHING

Use the quick-turn method for layering the quilt and finishing the edges, if you like, then quilt as desired. Or, you can quilt the layers and finish the raw edges with binding.

QUILTING IDEAS

Quilt as desired or use some of these ideas to enhance your quilt:

1. Stitch in the ditch around planes and borders.
2. Outline stitch inside the planes.
3. Quilt a 2"–2½" design across the wings.
4. Stitch a small design in the bodies of the planes.
5. Use an overall pattern or grid in the background.
6. A 2½"-wide quilting design can be used in the outer border.

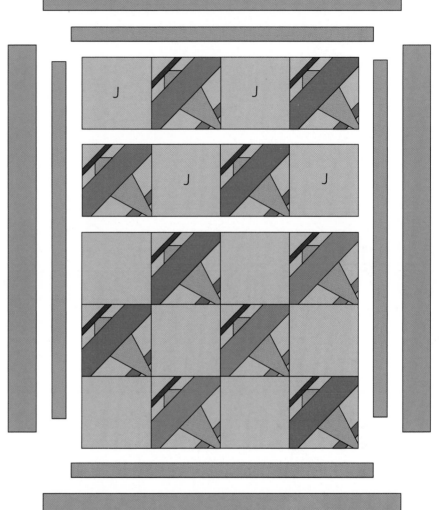

Quilt Assembly

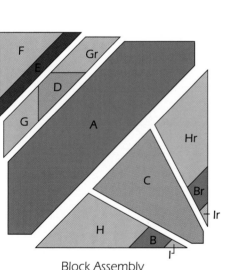

Block Assembly

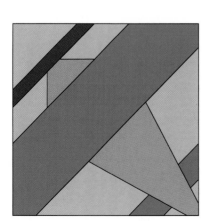

Completed Block

Need Help?	
Butted corners	p. 13
Chain piecing	p. 10
Half-square triangles	p. 9
Quick-turn finishing	p. 15
Rotary cutting	p. 8
Templates	p. 8

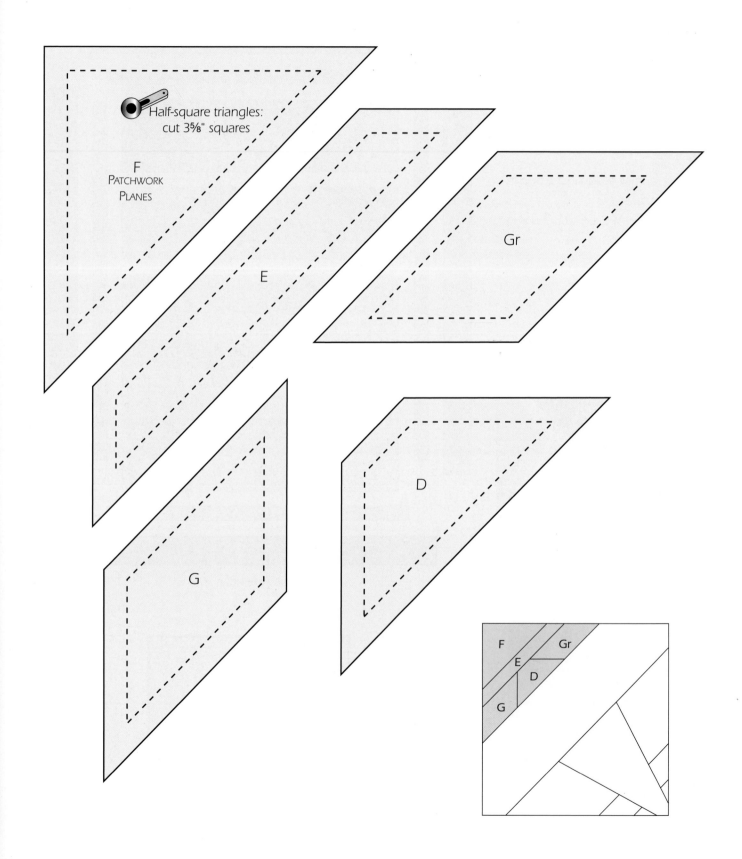

Half-square triangles:
cut 3⅝" squares

F
PATCHWORK
PLANES

E

Gr

G

D

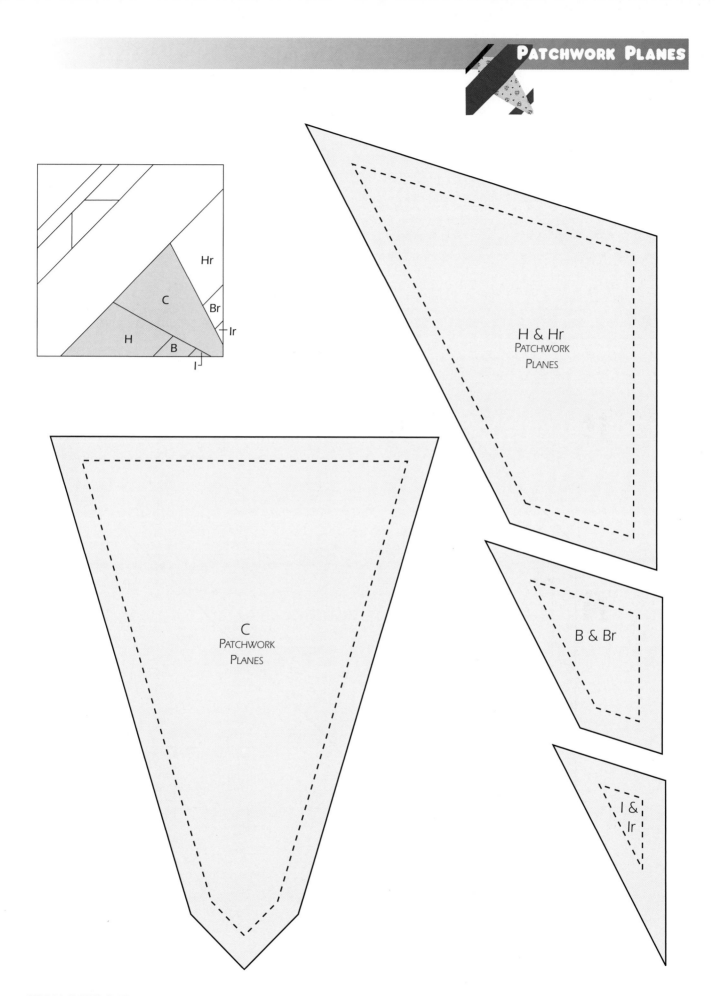

H & Hr
PATCHWORK
PLANES

C
PATCHWORK
PLANES

B & Br

I &
Ir

Hr

C

Br

Ir

H

B

I

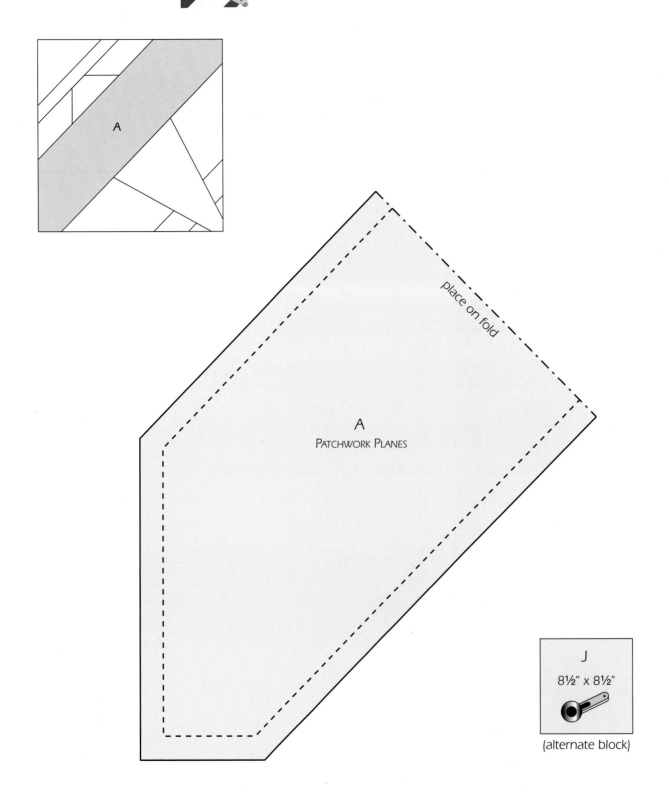

A
PATCHWORK PLANES

place on fold

J
8½" x 8½"

(alternate block)

WHICH WAY TO GO

I designed this quilt for a friend's son. My husband liked it so much that I made one for my son, too. As you can see, this quilt can be fun for children of all ages. The kids like to follow the arrows around the quilt, and I have seen cars, horses, dolls, and boats make the journey. Making the quilt is easier than you think, so I hope you will give it a try.

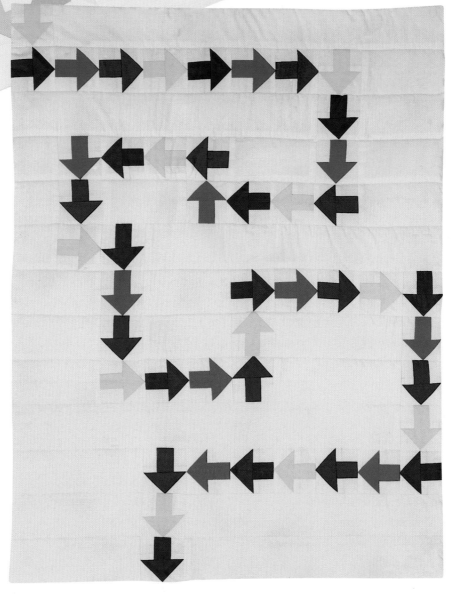

WHICH WAY TO GO

CUTTING INSTRUCTIONS
Quilt 40" x 52"
48 arrow blocks, 4" x 4"

FABRICS	YARDS	PATCHES
4 Arrow colors	¼ each	12 A, 12 C each color
Background	2¼	96 B, 96 D, 3 E, 11 F, 5 G, 2 H, 2 I, 2 J
Binding (optional)	½	2½" x 5½ yds.
Backing	1¾	1 panel 44" x 56"
	or 3⅜	2 panels 22½" x 56"
Batting		44" x 56"

CUTTING PATCHES

The Cutting Instructions show the number of patches to cut for each fabric.

SCISSOR CUTTING

Use the patterns on page 34 to make templates for the patches listed in the Cutting Instructions. Skip to Piecing Blocks.

ROTARY CUTTING

Rotary cutting dimensions are given in the patterns. Look for the rotary cutter symbol. The arrow points can be made with the quick-corner technique, and the tails can be strip pieced.

PIECING BLOCKS

Make 12 arrow-point units and 12 arrow-tail units for each color. There will be a ¼" overlap at the arrow points. Do not remove this. It is needed in the seam allowance. To finish the arrow blocks, stack the 2 units into separate piles by color.

Sew the arrow points and tails together, matching colors. You can use chain piecing to help speed this process, if you like.

ASSEMBLING QUILT

Starting with any color you want, put one block of each color in a stack. Continue to stack the arrows, placing the colors in the same order as the first four, until all have been put in the stack.

Since the arrows appear to be randomly placed on the quilt, the best way to get the arrows and background pieces where they belong is to lay them out, in order, on the floor or on a table before you start sewing. Check the Quilt Assembly diagram frequently for help. As the pieces are put in place, check the direction the arrows are pointing. When you have finished placing all the pieces, there will be 2 arrow blocks left over.

Sew the arrow blocks and background pieces together in rows. To help keep the rows in order, after sewing them, stack them or place them back on the floor or table in order. After all the rows have been sewn, sew the rows together in pairs, then sew the pairs together to complete the top.

FINISHING

Finish the quilt the quick-turn way. Then quilt as desired. Or, you can quilt the layers and finish the raw edges with binding.

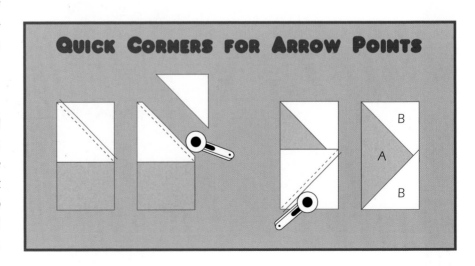

QUICK CORNERS FOR ARROW POINTS

QUILTING IDEAS

1. If you use a thick batting, you can quilt in the seam lines between the rows.
2. For a standard thickness of batting, quilt in the ditch or outline quilt inside or outside the arrows.
3. Use an overall pattern or grid in the background.

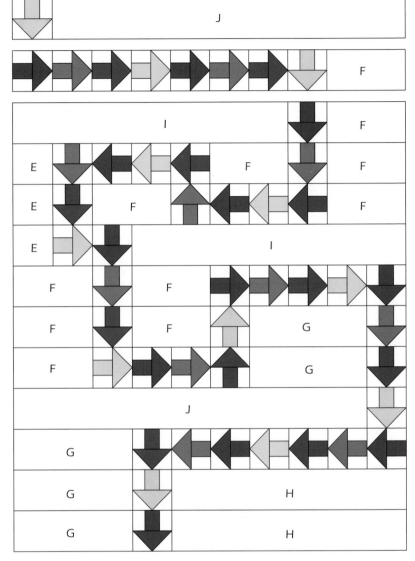

Quilt Assembly

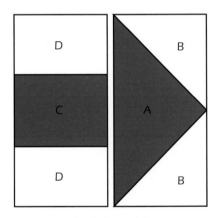

Block Assembly

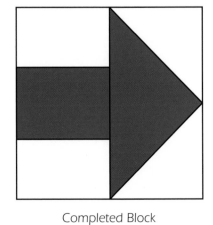

Completed Block

Need Help?	
Chain piecing	p. 10
Quick corner	p. 11
Quick-turn finishing	p. 15
Rotary cutting	p. 8
Strip piecing	p. 10
Templates	p. 8

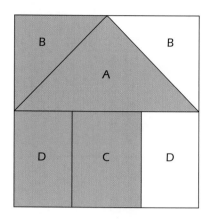

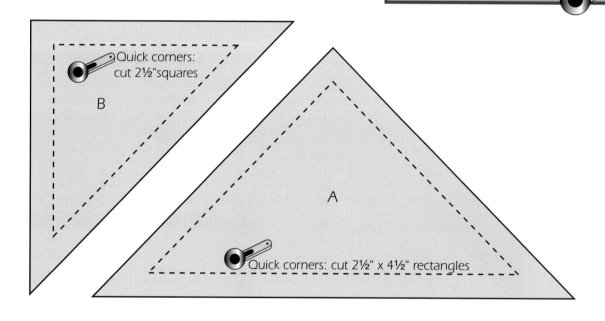

Quick corners: cut 2½"squares

Quick corners: cut 2½" x 4½" rectangles

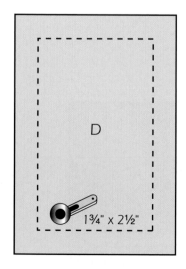

1¾" x 2½"

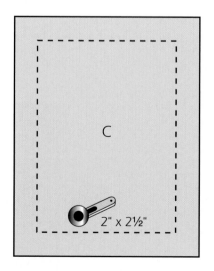

2" x 2½"

BUTTONED BUTTERFLIES

There is not one child I know who does not like to chase beautiful butterflies. This project will delight children and keep them busy buttoning and unbuttoning the wings of these festive butterflies.

Buttons are NOT recommended for infants or small children because buttons may present a choking hazard.

BUTTONED BUTTERFLIES

Cutting Instructions
Quilt 45½" x 45½"
18 butterfly blocks, 10" x 8"

Fabrics	Yards	Patches
Scraps (wings)	—	12 A, 12 Ar, 12 B, 12 Br, 6 C, 6 Cr, 6 D, 6 Dr
Lining (wings)	1½	12 A, 12 Ar, 12 B, 12 Br, 6 C, 6 Cr, 6 D, 6 Dr
Brown (bodies)	¼	18 I
Background	2	36 E, 18 F, 18 G 36 H, 36 J, 4M
Border 1 (mitered)	¼	4 strips 1¼" x 44½"
Border 2 (mitered)	½	4 strips 2½" x 48½"
Backing	3	2 panels 25½" x 49½"
Binding (optional)	½	2½" x 5½ yds.
Batting		49½" x 49½"

Supplies
Paint pen: black
Buttons: 36 size ¾" for upper wings
        36 size ⅞" for lower wings
        assorted sizes and colors for decoration

Cutting patches

The Cutting Instructions show the number of patches to cut for each fabric. Fabrics should be pre-washed.

Scissor cutting

Use the patterns on pages 40-42 to make templates for the patches listed in the Cutting Instructions. Skip to Piecing Blocks.

Rotary cutting

Rotary cutting dimensions are given in the patterns. Look for the rotary cutter symbol. Only the butterfly bodies and the background pieces can be rotary cut. Use the patterns on pages 40–41 to make templates for the butterfly wings.

Piecing blocks

Wings

Be sure to mark the button and buttonhole placements on the wing templates and on the wing patches. Lay out all four wings for each butterfly. Pin the appropriate wing lining to each wing, with right sides together. Leaving the straight edges unsewn, stitch around the outer edges of the wings with a ¼" seam allowance.

Clip the curves of the wings, almost to the seam line (Fig. 1). Turn the pieces right side out. Use your fingers to smooth the seams from the inside. Press the wing pieces. Top stitch ⅛" from the edge (Fig. 2).

If any decorative stitching or application of ribbon or lace is desired on the wings, this is the time to apply it. Wait to sew on decorative buttons until the quilt is finished.

Using the buttonhole placement indicated on the templates as your guide, sew the buttonholes in all the wing pieces. Cut the buttonhole openings and test them for size.

Note: The top stitching and buttonholes on the quilt shown in the photo were done with clear nylon thread. This type of thread was used so the stitching would not detract from the many colors used in the wings.

Bodies

Notice that the H triangles on the front of the body are smaller than the J triangles at the tail end. You can use the quick-corner method, as described on page 11, to add the H and J patches to the butterfly bodies. Add the F rectangles to the fronts of the bodies and the G rectangles to the tails.

Adding Wings

Place the wing sets in piles arranged like the finished butterflies. Be sure to stack the piles in the proper sewing order. There are 12 butterflies made with the A and B pieces and 6 butterflies made with C and D.

On a body unit, measure ¾" in from the seam at the head end (Fig. 3). With a pencil or a pin, mark this spot on both sides in the seam allowance. Then, measure ¾" in from the seam at the tail end and mark this spot on both sides. These marks are the wing placement guides. Mark all the body units this way.

Next, place an upper wing on top of a body unit, right sides together (Fig. 4). Align the top edge of the wing with the mark at the head end. Staystitch the wing ⅛" in from the edge (Fig. 4).

Place a lower wing on the body unit, right sides together. Align the bottom edge of the wing with the mark at the tail end. The lower wing piece will overlap the upper wing piece (Fig. 5). Staystitch the wing in place as before. Repeat the process to attach the wings to the other side of the butterfly. Attach the wings to the 18 body units.

Sew an E rectangle to each side of the body units (see Butterfly Assembly diagrams on page 39). While sewing the seams, when you reach the area where the wings are attached, backstitch over the wing edges and on the area in the center where the wings overlap. The backstitches will help prevent the wings from pulling out during use. Attach the E's to all the butterflies to complete the blocks.

After piecing and pressing the blocks, trace the antennae (page 40) on each butterfly block and go over the tracings with a paint pen. You can practice on a scrap first. Allow the paint to dry before assembling the quilt top.

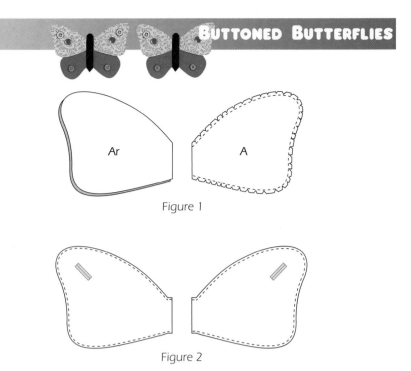

Figure 1

Figure 2

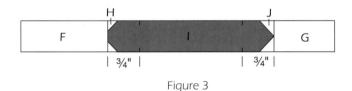

Figure 3

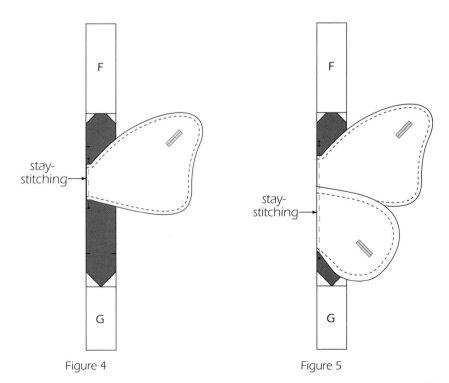

Figure 4

Figure 5

Detail of Buttoned Butterflies

Need Help?

Mitered corners	p. 13
Chain piecing	p. 10
Quick-turn finishing	p. 15
Rotary cutting	p. 8
Templates	p. 8

ASSEMBLING QUILT

Following the Quilt Assembly diagram, lay the blocks out on a flat surface in the order you would like them. Sew the blocks together across the quilt, then sew the rows together.

ADDING BORDERS

If your inner border fabric is at least 43½" wide (without selvages), you can cut four 1¼"-wide strips across the fabric to use for Border 1. If the fabric is not wide enough, cut 5 strips and splice them as needed to make four 43½" lengths. The outer border strips will also need to be spliced to make the 48½" lengths.

Matching centers, sew an inner border to each outer border lengthwise. Sew all four combined borders to the quilt, leaving the ¼" seam allowances unsewn at the corners. Be sure to begin and end each line of stitching with a backstitch to anchor the threads. Then miter all four corners. Trim the extra length along the miters, leaving a ¼" seam allowance, which can be pressed open.

FINISHING

This quilt will need to be layered and quilted before sewing the buttons. After quilting the top and finishing the edges, sew the wing buttons and the decorative buttons. The ¾" buttons are for the upper wings and the ⅞" buttons are for the lower wings.

When the buttons are securely sewn in place and the wings are buttoned down, the wings should lie flat and smooth, without stretching or buckling. Continue to sew decorative buttons to the wings anywhere you like. Please sew all buttons extremely well, using strong thread. If this quilt will be in the hands of a child, it is very important to attach all buttons securely. If any buttons come loose during use, resew them immediately. Loose buttons can present a choking hazard to small children.

QUILTING IDEAS

1. Quilt in the ditch around the butterfly bodies and borders.
2. Quilt an overall design or grid in the background.
3. Stitch a 1½" design in the outer border.

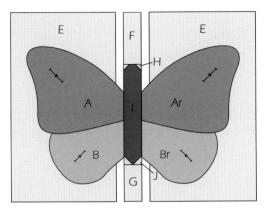

Butterfly 1 Assembly

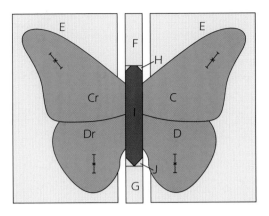

Butterfly 2 Assembly

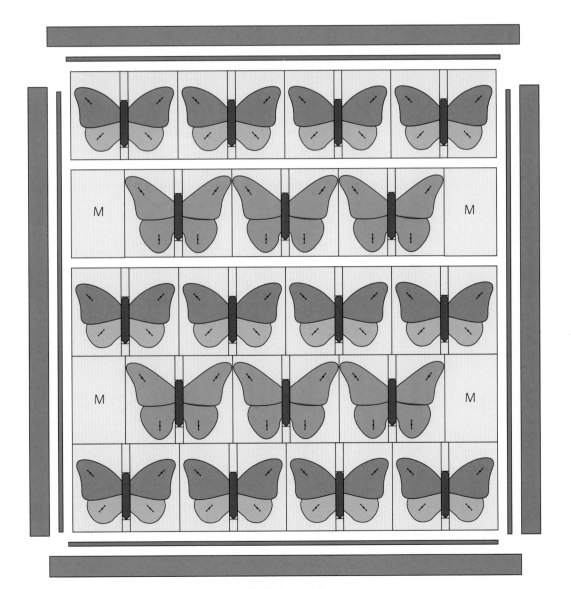

Quilt Assembly

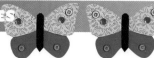

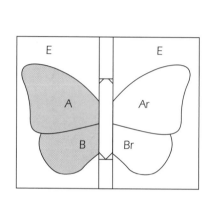

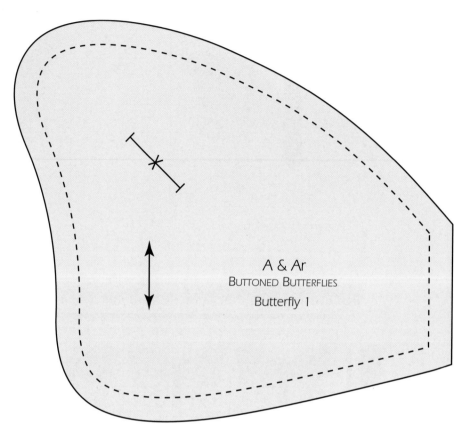

A & Ar
BUTTONED BUTTERFLIES
Butterfly 1

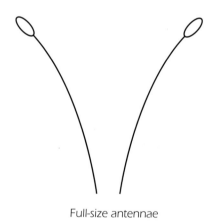

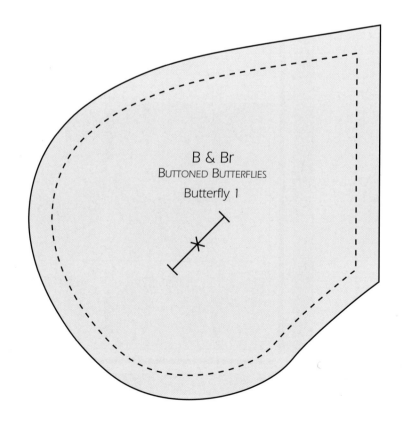

B & Br
BUTTONED BUTTERFLIES
Butterfly 1

Full-size antennae

40

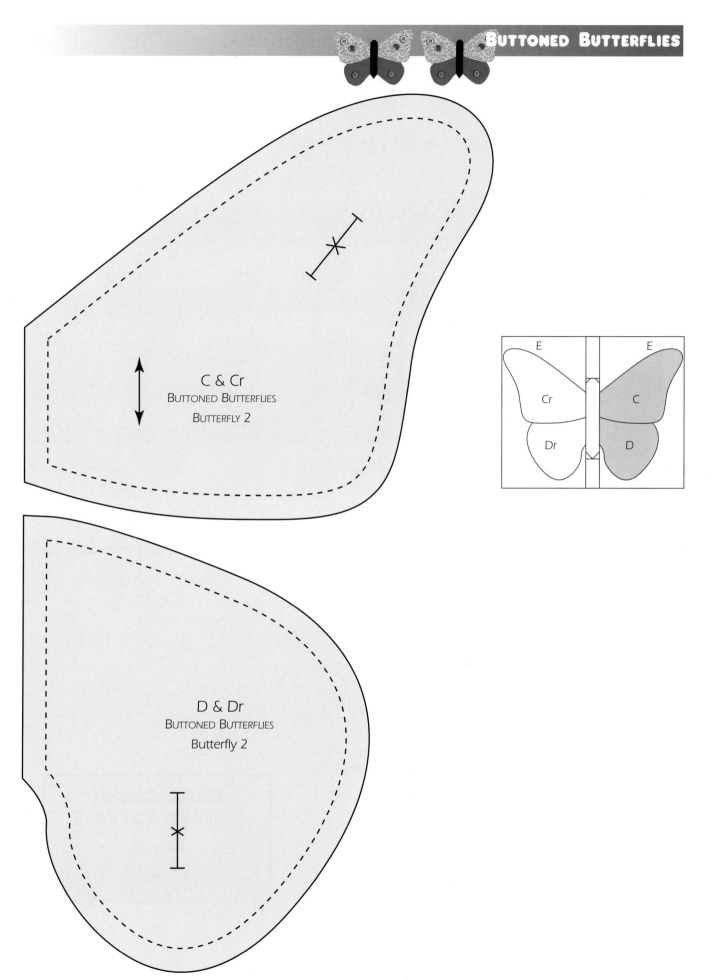

C & Cr
BUTTONED BUTTERFLIES
BUTTERFLY 2

D & Dr
BUTTONED BUTTERFLIES
Butterfly 2

E   E

Cr   C

Dr   D

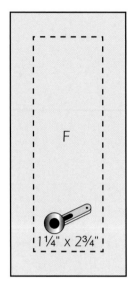

F

1¼" x 2¾"

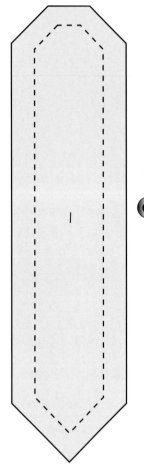

I

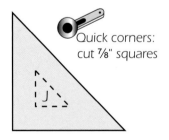

Quick corners:
cut 1¼"x 4¾" rectangles

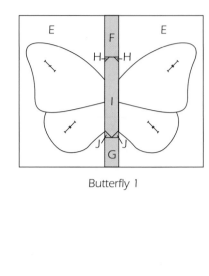

Butterfly 1

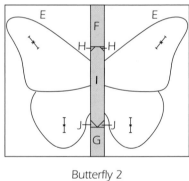

Butterfly 2

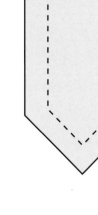

G

1¼" x 2"

J

Quick corners:
cut ⅞" squares

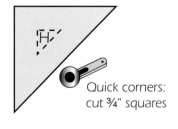

H

Quick corners:
cut ¾" squares

BACKGROUND ROTARY PATCHES

E   8½" x 5⅛"

M   8½" x 5½"

CHIEF SILVER CLOUD

Inspiration for this quilt comes from the story of a Great-great-uncle Silver Cloud in our family. Children like this quilt because it's fun, and they get a lot of practice tying bows. A surprise can be hidden in each tepee, and you will be pleased by how easy it is to sew the tepees.

CHIEF SILVER CLOUD, hand quilted by Alecia Knox

CUTTING INSTRUCTIONS

Quilt 42" x 54"

9 tepee blocks, 10" x 10"

1 campfire block, 10" x 10"

12 arrows, 3" x 6"; 12 canoes, 3" x 6"; 4 thunderbirds, 3" x 3"

Fabrics	Yards	Patches
Scraps	—	
* tepees (flaps and linings)		18 A, 18 Ar, 9 B
campfire		1 Y, 1 Z, 1 AA, 2 CC
Block backgrounds	1⅝	9 C, 9 Cr, 15 D, 1 BB, 1 DD, 2 EE, 1 FF, 4 GG
White	⅜	
arrows		12 E
canoes		24 L, 12 M, 12 Mr, 12 O
Red	¼	
arrows		12 G, 12 I, 12 Ir
thunderbirds		4 Q, 4 T, 4 U, 4 V, 4 X, 4 Xr
Border background	⅞	
arrows		12 F, 12 Fr, 12 H, 12 Hr 24 J, 24 K
canoes		48 L, 12 M, 12 Mr 12 N, 24 P
thunderbirds		4 R, 8 S, 8 U, 4 W, 4Wr 4 X, 4 Xr
Outer border (butted)	¾	
		2 strips 3½" x 57" 2 strips 3½" x 39"
Backing	2¾	2 panels 29½" x 46"
Binding (optional)	½	2½" x 5⅝ yds.
Batting		46" x 58"

Supplies
9 shoelaces, at least 12" long
Thread sealant
Wax paper
6 yds. of ½", single fold, commercial bias tape for tepee poles
*Prewash the fabrics for the tepees to prevent shrinkage.

CUTTING PATCHES

The Cutting Instructions show the number of patches to cut for each of the fabrics.

SCISSOR CUTTING

Use the patterns on pages 50-54 to make templates for the patches listed under the Cutting Instructions. Skip to Piecing Blocks.

ROTARY CUTTING

Rotary cutting dimensions are given in the patterns. Look for the rotary cutter symbol. For the J patches (arrows) and L patches (canoes), use the rotary cutting dimensions to make squares. Then cut the squares in half diagonally to make the half-square triangles. You will need templates for patterns that do not have the rotary cutter symbol.

SHOELACES

Cut 5½" from each end of every shoelace. Discard the center portions, keeping the finished ends. You will have 18 pieces, two for each tepee. Coat the cut ends with thread sealant and lay the shoelaces on wax paper to dry.

BIAS TAPE

Cut 18 pieces 12" long for the tepee poles, two pieces for each tepee.

PIECING BLOCKS
TEPEE BLOCKS

Select a set of tepee flaps and linings (2 A and 2 Ar). Place the linings so they are right side up with the center edges facing each other.

On both pieces, measure 3¼" up from the bottom, along the center edge (Fig. 1). In the seam allowances, mark this measurement with a pencil. Center the cut end of a shoelace on this mark for each flap, extending the ends beyond the pattern pieces by ¼". Stitch the ends of the shoelaces in place in the seam allowance.

Place the tepee flaps on top of the linings, with right sides together. They should line up exactly. Stitch a pair together with a ¼" seam allowance, except for the outside angled edge which should be left unsewn. When you sew across a shoelace, stop and backstitch over it to secure it in place. After sewing the three edges, trim the two inside corners and clip the curves (Fig. 2). Turn the flap right side out and press. Top stitch the sewn edges ⅛" in from the edge. Repeat for the other flap. Make 9 right flaps and 9 left flaps. If any other decorative stitching is desired, this is the time to add it.

Next, place a B tepee piece right side up. Lay two tepee flaps on top, also right side up. Align the slanted edges, placing the flaps ¼" from the top and bottom of B. If there is a gap in the center where the two flaps meet, move the flaps toward the center until there is no space between them. Stay-stitch the flaps in place along the outside slanted edges, ⅛" from the edges. See Fig. 3 for the placement of these pieces.

Sew the C and Cr background pieces to the sides of the tepee with a ¼" seam allowance. This seam will catch the tepee flaps. Press the seam allowances toward B and sew the D patch to the block. Be careful not to catch the tops of flaps in this seam.

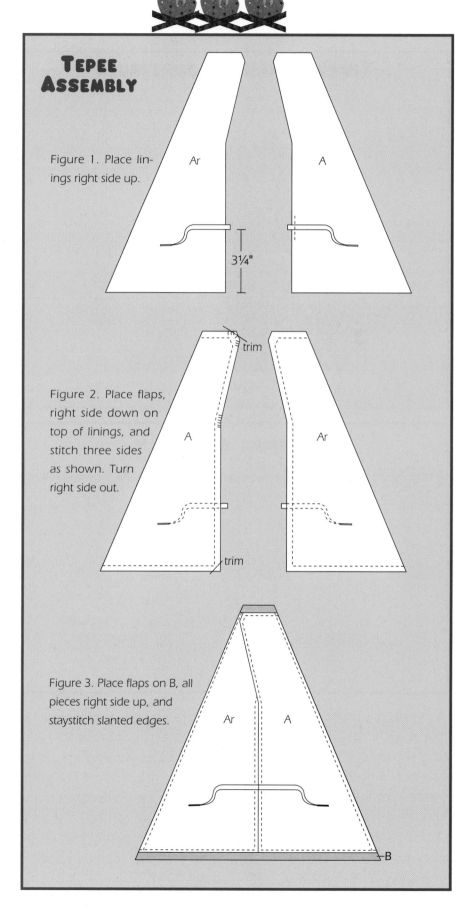

TEPEE ASSEMBLY

Figure 1. Place linings right side up.

Ar   A

3¼"

Figure 2. Place flaps, right side down on top of linings, and stitch three sides as shown. Turn right side out.

trim   A   Ar   trim

Figure 3. Place flaps on B, all pieces right side up, and staystitch slanted edges.

Ar   A   B

TEPEE ASSEMBLY CONTINUED

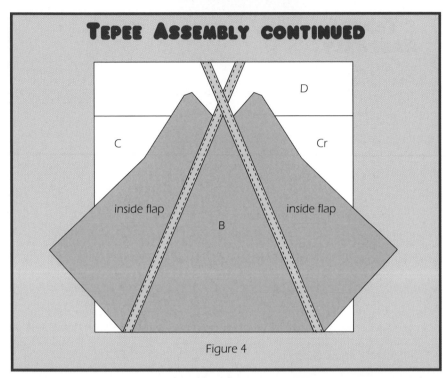

D

C

Cr

inside flap   inside flap

B

Figure 4

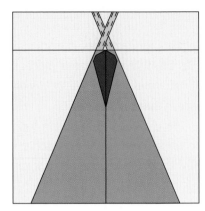

Completed Tepee Block

CAMPFIRE ASSEMBLY

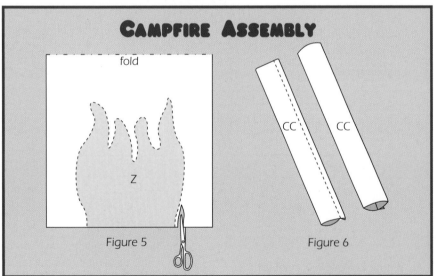

fold

Z

CC   CC

Figure 5   Figure 6

Finish the block with the bias-tape tepee poles: Open the tepee flaps and lay one piece of the bias tape face up on the B piece, running from the top to bottom of the block along the flap seam (Fig. 4). Top stitch close to the edge of the tape on both sides. Repeat this process with the other piece of tape, crossing it over the first bias strip at the top of the tepee. Trim any excess length even with the edges of the block.

When finished, the top of the flaps can be folded back and tacked at the top to hold them open. Use the guide marks on the B template for this step. Make 9 tepee blocks.

CAMPFIRE

Another tepee block or a solid 10½" square of the background fabric can be substituted for the campfire block, if you like.

For the Z flame, fold the 5" x 10" strip in half, right sides together, to form a 5" square. Place the bottom of the Z template on the edge of the square opposite the fold and trace. Pin the fabric layers together both inside and outside the traced lines and sew on the line.

Carefully trim the excess fabric away (Fig. 5), leaving a ⅛" seam allowance, by eye, all around. Clip the curves and turn the piece right side out. Press the piece and top stitch around it close to the edge, but leave the bottom open. Repeat for the Y (5½" x 11" rectangle) and AA (4" x 8" rectangle) flames.

Fold the CC pieces for the campfire logs in half down the length of each piece, wrong sides together. Stitch with a ¼" seam allowance along the full length of the pieces, creating tubes. Lay the tubes on an ironing board and roll them over their seams until the seams are completely covered by the tubes. Then press the tubes (Fig. 6).

Make a dot ¼" in from each corner of the BB piece. Use the marks as guides for placing the logs in an X, from one corner to the opposite corner (Fig. 7). Do not sew the logs just yet.

Place the Y flame under the edges of the logs. Be sure the unsewn edge of the flame is completely covered by the logs. (Approximately ¼" to ⅜" of the flame should be covered.) Pin the flame in place. Remove the logs and staystitch the bottom edge of the flame to the BB piece. Next, replace one of the logs and stitch in place along both edges. Sew the second log in place.

Align the bottom edge of the Z flame with the bottom edge of the DD rectangle (Fig. 8). Staystitch in place. Sew DD to the top of BB. The Z flame will be sewn into the seam between the two pieces.

To add the third flame, place the AA piece along the top edge of the DD piece. Just push the other flames out of the way. Stay-stitch the AA in place to complete the campfire unit (Fig. 9).

Sew both the EE pieces to the campfire unit (see the Block Assembly diagram on the next page). Stitch the FF piece to the top of the campfire unit. This step sews the AA flame into the seam. To finish this block, attach the D rectangle to the bottom of the campfire unit.

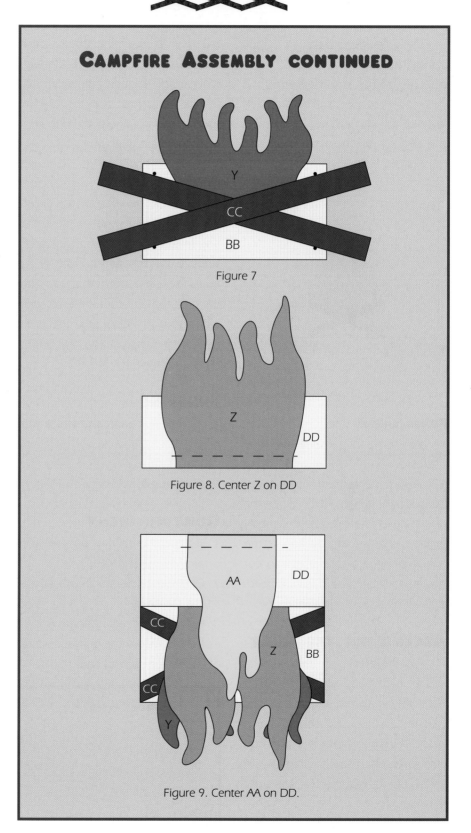

CAMPFIRE ASSEMBLY CONTINUED

Figure 7

Figure 8. Center Z on DD

Figure 9. Center AA on DD.

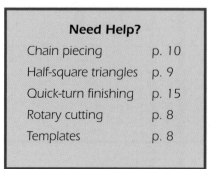

Use a needle and thread to tack down the flames as indicated by the plus (+) signs on the template pieces. Sew through only the back layer of the flame fabric. That way, the thread will not show on the front of the flames.

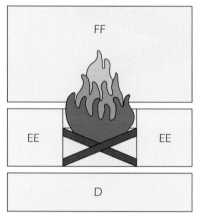

Campfire Block Assembly

PIECED BORDER

Referring to the assembly diagrams on pages 50 and 51, make 12 arrows, 12 canoes, and 4 thunderbirds. Please note that, when the arrow head has been sewn, the H and Hr patches will overlap at the arrow point. Be careful not to cut this area off because it will be needed later as a seam allowance.

ASSEMBLING THE QUILT

Lay the blocks on a flat surface in the order shown in the Quilt Assembly diagram. First, sew the canoe, arrow, and thunderbird blocks together for the top and bottom rows. Then sew the canoe and arrow blocks together for the sides of the quilt.

Sew the tepee blocks, campfire block, and GG background pieces together to make the three vertical rows. Sew the three rows together, then attach the two side rows. Add the canoe, arrow, and thunderbird rows to the top and bottom to complete the main quilt area.

Cut 5 border strips 3½" wide from selvage to selvage. Splice these pieces as needed to create the border lengths given in the Cutting Instructions. Attach the shortest strips to the top and bottom of the quilt. Press the borders away from the quilt top and trim the ends even with the quilt edge. Sew the other two border strips to the side edges. Press and trim.

FINISHING

Finish the quilt the quick-turn way. Then quilt as desired. Or, you can quilt the layers and finish the raw edges with binding.

QUILTING IDEAS

1. Stitch in the ditch or outline quilt around the tepees.
2. Quilt wavy lines for smoke above the campfire.
3. If you have used a print in the border, follow the printed pattern with your quilting lines.

Need Help?	
Chain piecing	p. 10
Half-square triangles	p. 9
Quick-turn finishing	p. 15
Rotary cutting	p. 8
Templates	p. 8

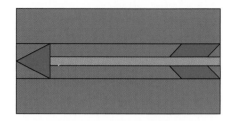

Completed Arrow Block

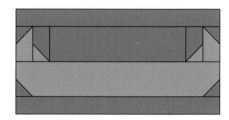

Completed Canoe Block

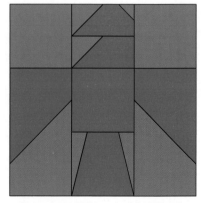

Completed Thunderbird Block

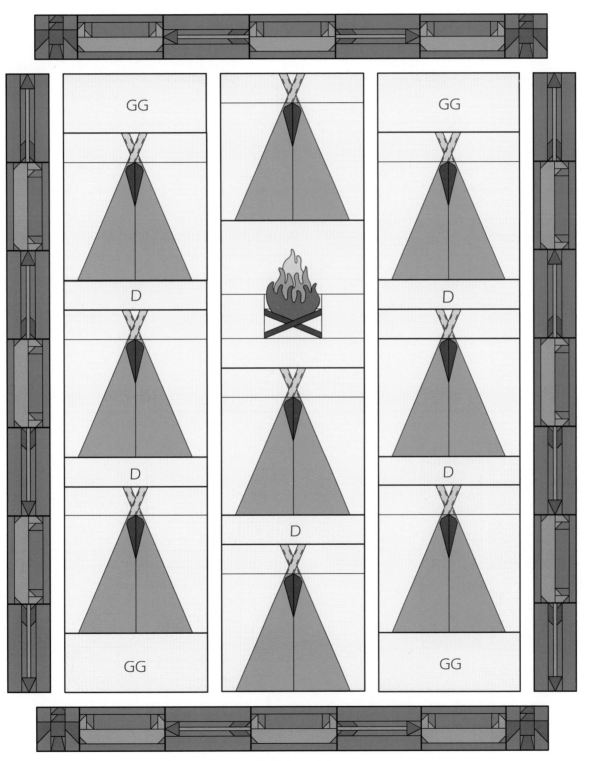

Quilt Assembly

ROTARY PATCHES

E ¾" x 5½"

J 1¼" x 1¼" (h.s.)

K 1½" x 6½"

h.s. = half-square triangles

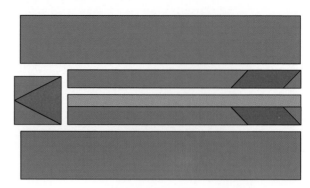

Arrow Assembly

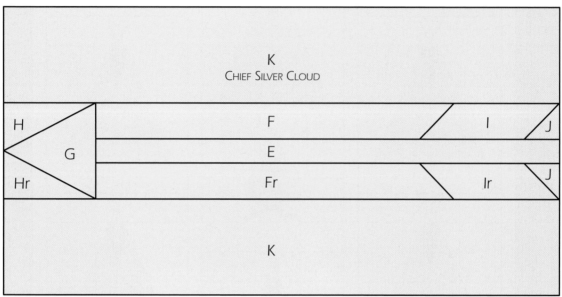

K

CHIEF SILVER CLOUD

H

G

Hr

F

E

Fr

I

J

Ir

J

K

Full-size pattern. Add seam allowances.

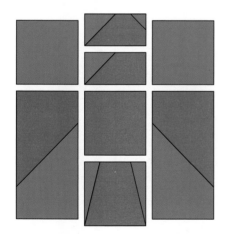

Thunderbird Assembly

ROTARY PATCHES

R 1⅛" x 1⅛" (h.s.)

S 1⅜" x 1⅜" (h.s.)

U 1½" x 1½"

h.s. = half-square triangles

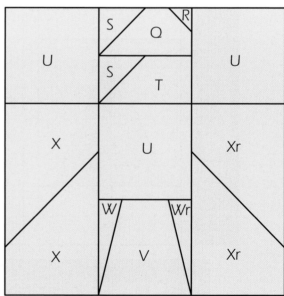

R

S

Q

U

U

S

T

X

U

Xr

W

Wr

X

V

Xr

Full-size pattern. Add seam allowances.

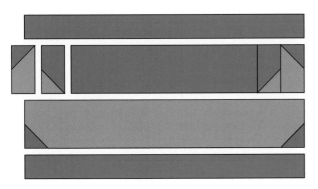

Canoe Assembly

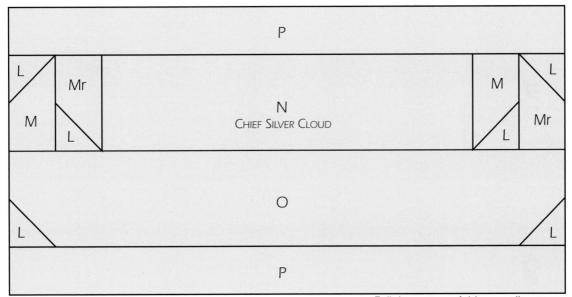

Full-size pattern. Add seam allowances.

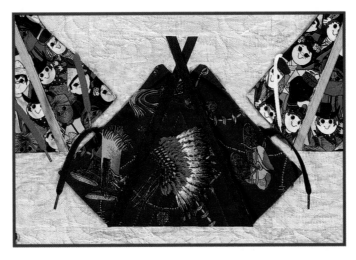

Detail of tepees

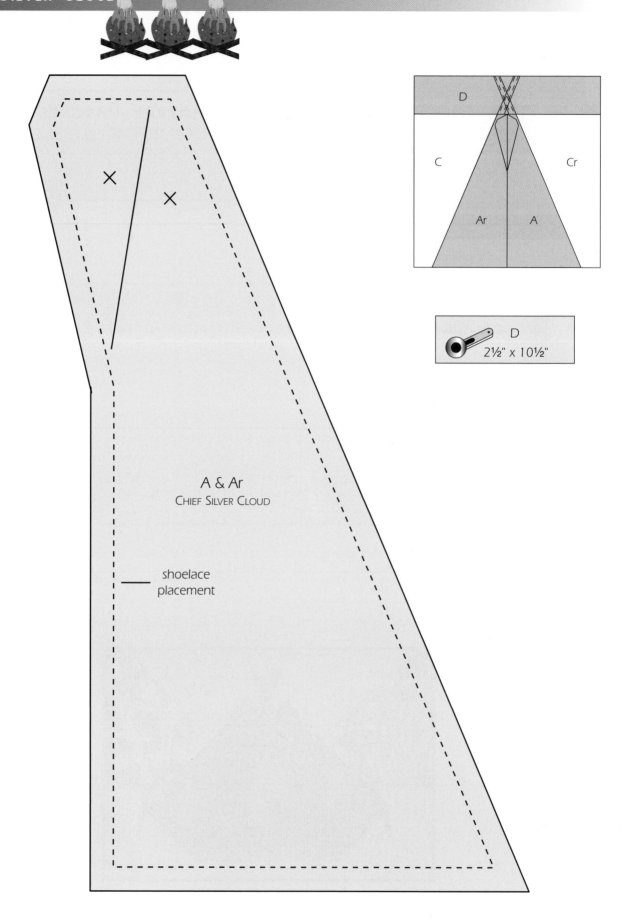

D

C   Cr

Ar   A

D
2½" x 10½"

A & Ar
CHIEF SILVER CLOUD

—— shoelace
placement

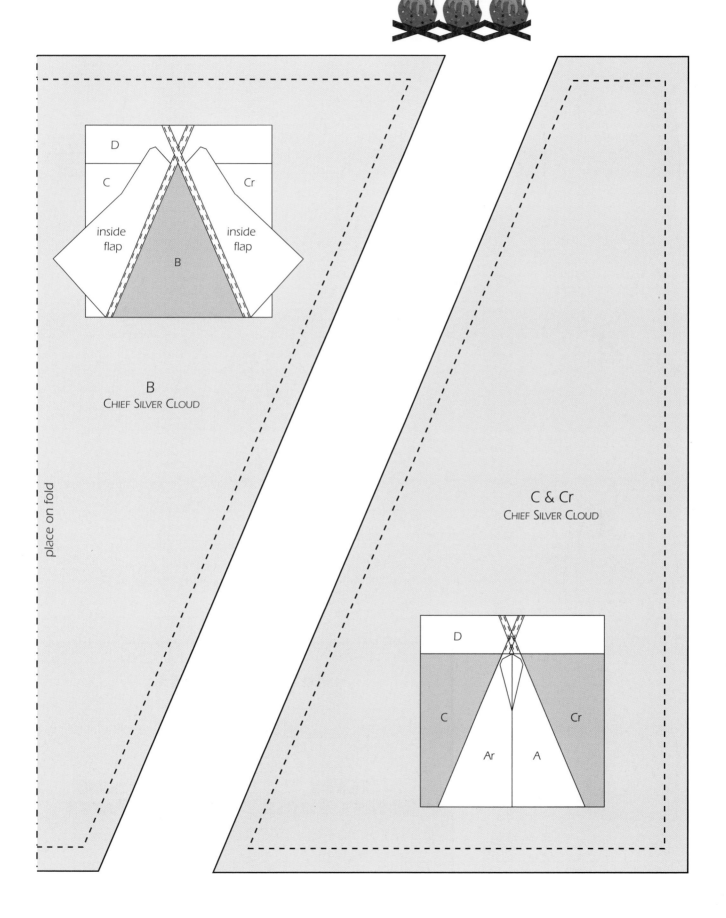

B
CHIEF SILVER CLOUD

C & Cr
CHIEF SILVER CLOUD

place on fold

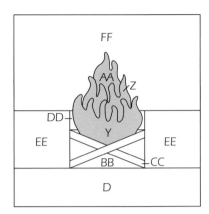

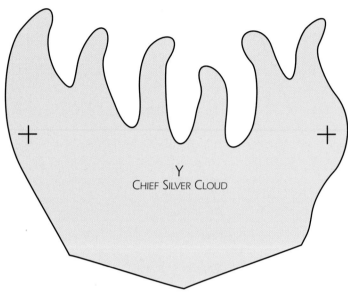

Y
CHIEF SILVER CLOUD

Z
CHIEF SILVER CLOUD

AA
CHIEF SILVER CLOUD

CAMPFIRE ROTARY PATCHES

BB 2½" x 4½"   EE 3½" x 3½"
CC 1¼" x 5½"   FF 5½" x 10½"
DD ½" x 4½"

FLAME ROTARY PIECES

AA 4" x 8"
Z   5" x 10"
Y   5½" x 11"

BACKGROUND ROTARY PATCH

GG 4½" x 10½"

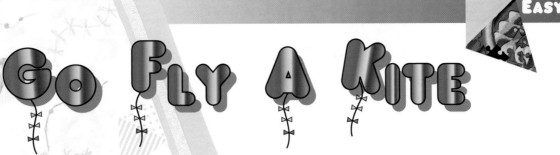

Go Fly A Kite

Remember those windy days in the park when we went to fly our kites? Kites are still favorite toys for children today, and they enjoy them as much as we did. This quilt will delight any child and remind them of a beautiful day in the park as they watched kites swirl through the air.

Buttons are NOT recommended for infants and small children because buttons may present a choking hazard.

Go Fly a Kite, hand quilting by Leesa Loyd

CUTTING INSTRUCTIONS
Quilt 45½" x 45½"

10 kite blocks, 6" x 6"

FABRICS	YARDS	PATCHES
Scraps (kites)	—	2 A, 5 C, 5 D, 6 E, 3 F, 3 Fr
Background	1½	10 B, 10 Br, 26 G
Border 1 (butted)	¼	2 strips 1¼" x 40" 2 strips 1¼" x 38½"
Border 2 (butted)	⅜	2 strips 1¾" x 42½" 2 strips 1¾" x 40"
Border 3 (butted)	⅝	2 strips 3¼" x 48" 2 strips 3¼" x 42½"
Backing	3	2 panels 25¼" x 49½"
Binding (optional)	½	2½" x 5⅜ yds.
Batting		49½" x 49½"

SUPPLIES
⅛" wide ribbon: 12½" for buttons or, if using bows, 1½ yds. for each kite
Thread sealant
Wax paper
Assorted buttons, approx. 6 per kite (optional)

CUTTING PATCHES
The Cutting Instructions show the number of patches to cut for each of the fabrics.

SCISSOR CUTTING
Use the patterns on pages 58-60 to make templates for patches listed in the Cutting Instructions. Skip to Piecing Blocks.

ROTARY CUTTING
Only the G patch, a 6½" square, can be rotary cut. You will need templates for the rest of the patches.

RIBBONS
Cut 10 pieces of ribbon 12½" long for the kite tails. Some kite tails can be decorated with buttons and some with bows. For each kite with bows, cut 6 ribbon pieces 6½" long. Coat the cut ends with thread sealant to help keep the ribbons from coming apart in the wash. Lay them out on wax paper to dry. Tie each 6½" ribbon in a bow.

PIECING BLOCKS
There are 3 different kites. Fol-

low the Block Assembly diagrams to make 10 kite blocks. On each block, pin a 12½" length of ribbon to the tail of the kite (Fig. 1). Staystitch the end of the ribbon in the seam allowance. Leave the rest of the ribbon pinned to the kite so it will be out of the way when you sew the blocks together.

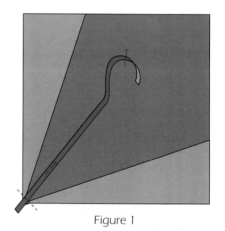

Figure 1

ASSEMBLING QUILT
Using the 10 kite blocks and 26 solid blocks (G patches), lay the pieces on a flat surface in 6 rows of 6 blocks. You can follow the Quilt Assembly diagram, or you can position your kites however you like.

Sew the blocks together into rows. Then sew the rows together. The ribbons will be caught in the seams.

ADDING BORDERS
All of the borders have butted corners. Sew the shortest Border 1 strips to the sides of the quilt first. Cut off the extra length even with the top and bottom of the quilt and press. Then sew the remaining Bor-

der 1 strips to the top and bottom. Trim and press as before. Repeat these steps for Border 2. For Border 3, you will need to cut five 3¼" strips from selvage to selvage. Then splice the strips as needed to create the lengths given in the Cutting Instructions. Sew the strips to the quilt as for the first two borders.

FINISHING

Finish the quilt the quick-turn way. Then quilt as desired. Or, you can quilt the layers and finish the raw edges with binding.

After the quilting is complete, the buttons and bows can be securely attached as follows: Arrange the kite-tail ribbons in curves, twisting the ribbons once in a while. At approximately 1½" to 2" intervals, place a pin to hold the ribbons in place and to mark the spots where a button or bow will be attached.

After pinning all the ribbons, stop and look at the placement. Do the kites look like they are moving? They should make smooth curves that mimic the tracks of flying kites. If not, you can rearrange the ribbons.

When you are happy with the arrangement, use heavy thread to attach the buttons and bows, sewing through the ribbons. For the bows, sew through the center knots so the bows will not come untied.

QUILTING IDEAS

1. Quilt in the ditch around each of the kites.
2. Use a free-hand flowing pattern in the background to simulate clouds.
3. Stitch concentric diamon shapes or radiating lines inside the kites.

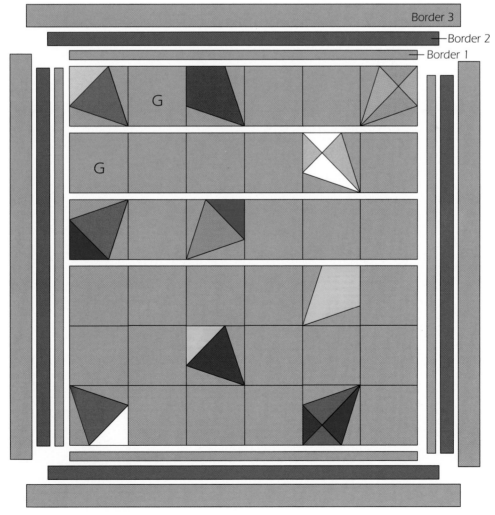

Quilt Assembly

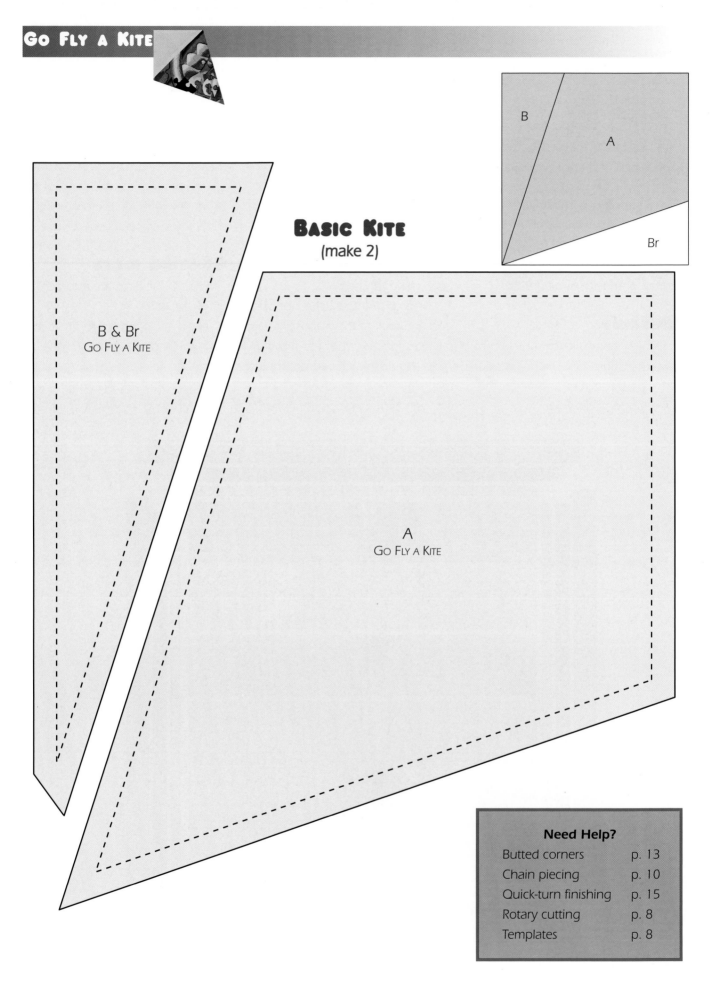

BASIC KITE
(make 2)

B

A

Br

B & Br
GO FLY A KITE

A
GO FLY A KITE

Need Help?

Butted corners	p. 13
Chain piecing	p. 10
Quick-turn finishing	p. 15
Rotary cutting	p. 8
Templates	p. 8

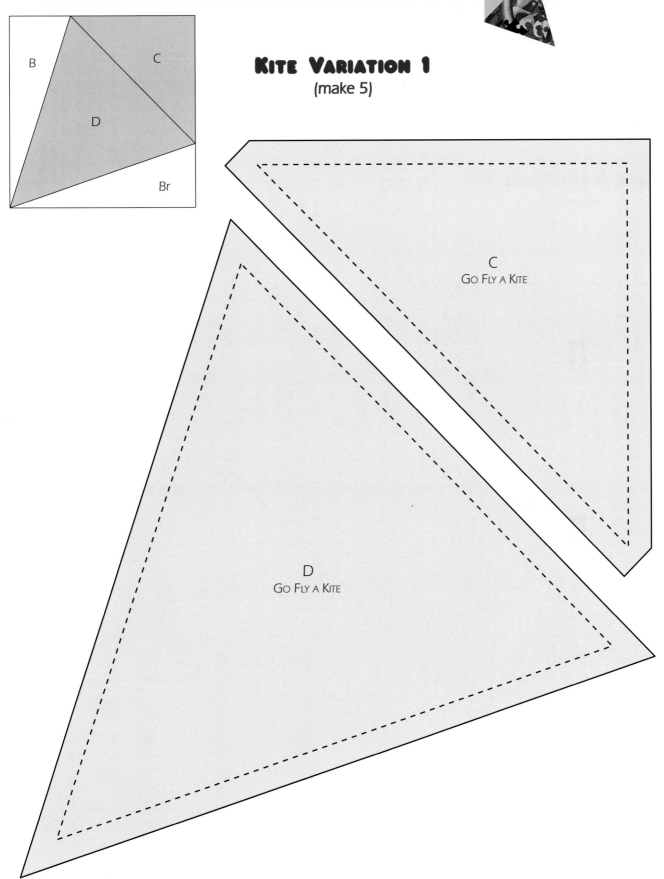

KITE VARIATION 1
(make 5)

STITCH A CHILD'S QUILT, Vicki M. A. Thomas

KITE VARIATION 2
(make 3)

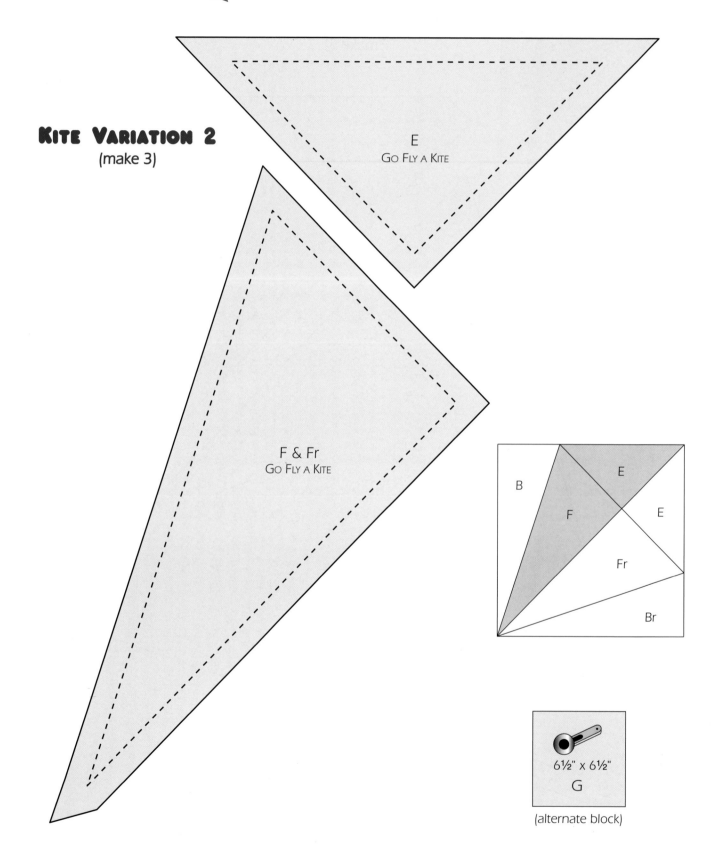

E
GO FLY A KITE

F & Fr
GO FLY A KITE

B

E

F

E

Fr

Br

6½" x 6½"
G

(alternate block)

PAPER DOLLS

Remember cutting paper dolls and hearts when you were small? Children still thrill at making them. They are fascinated by the trick of folding paper and making a few simple scissor cuts to create a chain of figures or designs.

PAPER DOLLS, hand quilted by Alecia Knox

CUTTING INSTRUCTIONS

Quilt 44" x 58"

12 girl dolls, 6" x 8", 12 boy dolls, 6" x 8"

27 hearts, 4" x 4"

FABRICS	YARDS (for one row)	PATCHES (for one row)
Doll blocks		
girl dolls	⅜	6 A, 6 D, 6 E, 6 G
girl background	⅜	24 B, 12 C, 6 F, 6 Fr, 6 H, 6 Hr
boy dolls	⅜	6 A, 6 C, 6 D, 6 I, 6 Ir, 12 L
boy background	⅜	24 B, 24 C, 12 J 12 Jr, 12 K
Heart blocks	¼	9 N, 9 Nr
background	¼	36 O, 18 P

	YARDS (for quilt shown)	PIECES (for quilt shown)
Sashing	⅝	
row sashes		8 strips 1½" x 36½"
side sashes		2 strips 1½" x 54½"
Border (butted)	⅝	2 strips 3½" x 60½" 2 strips 3½" x 40½"
Backing	2⅞	2 panels 31½" x 48"
Binding (optional)	⅝	2½" x 6 yds.
Batting		48" x 62"

CUTTING PATCHES

Yardage is given by row, so you can use as many rows of each block in as many color combinations as you would like.

SCISSORS

Use the patterns on pages 64-66 to make templates for the patches listed in the Cutting Instructions. Skip to Piecing Blocks.

ROTARY CUTTER

Rotary cutting dimensions are given in the patterns. Look for the symbol. Leave patches A, B, O, and P as squares to use for the quick-corner technique. If you use half-square triangles, add ⅜" to the measurements for the quick-corner squares. You need templates for patterns that do not have the rotary symbol.

PIECING BLOCKS

To make the quilt shown in the photo, refer to the Block Assembly diagrams and make 12 girl doll blocks, 12 boy doll blocks, and 27 heart blocks.

ASSEMBLING QUILT

Sew the paper dolls in rows of 6 blocks each and the hearts in rows of 9 each. Measure the rows to make sure they are 36½" long. If they are not, make adjustments in the seam allowances between the blocks.

Lay the rows out on a flat surface in sewing order. Add a 1½" x 36½" sashing strip to the bottom of each row and the top of the first row. Then sew all the rows together.

Sew a 1½" x 54½" sashing strip to each side of the quilt and trim off extra length.

ADDING BORDERS

Stitch the short border strips to the top and bottom of the quilt and trim off the extra length. Then add the long borders to the sides of the quilt and trim.

FINISHING

Finish the quilt the quick-turn way. Then quilt as desired. Alternatively, you can quilt the layers and then finish the raw edges with binding.

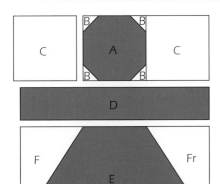

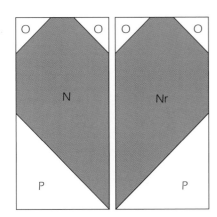

Girl Block Assembly

QUILTING IDEAS

1. Outline quilt the dolls ¼" inside the seam lines.
2. Stitch little hearts on the girls' dresses and in the backgrounds between the boys.
3. Stitch in the seams on both sides of each sashing strip, including the long side pieces.
4. Quilt a simple 2" to 2½"-wide braid or grid pattern in the border.

Need Help?	
Butted corners	p. 13
Chain piecing	p. 10
Quick corners	p. 11
Quick-turn finishing	p. 15
Rotary cutting	p. 8
Templates	p. 8

Heart Block Assembly

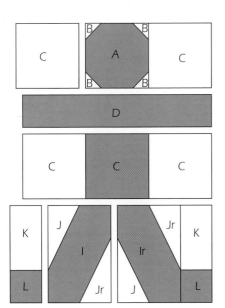

Boy Block Assembly

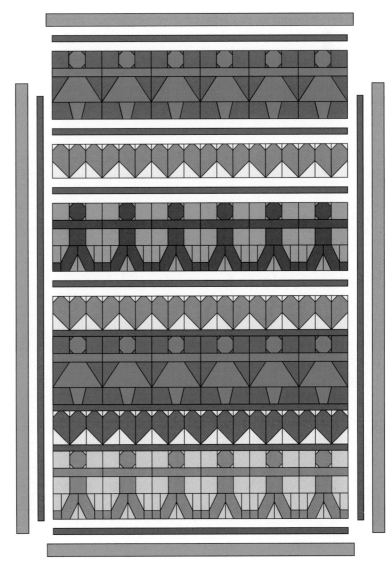

Quilt Assembly

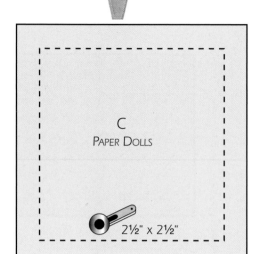

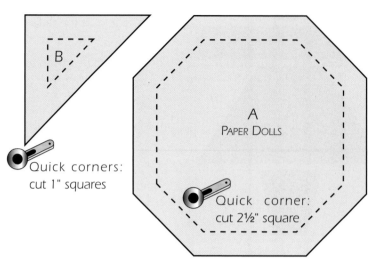

C
PAPER DOLLS

B

2½" x 2½"

Quick corners:
cut 1" squares

A
PAPER DOLLS

Quick corner:
cut 2½" square

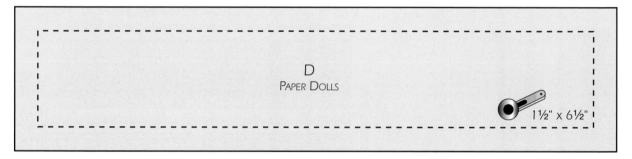

D
PAPER DOLLS

1½" x 6½"

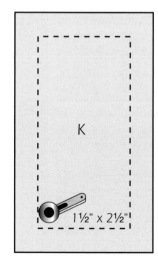

K

1½" x 2½"

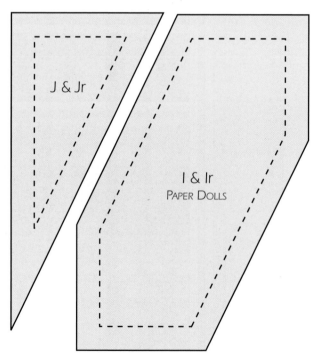

J & Jr

I & Ir
PAPER DOLLS

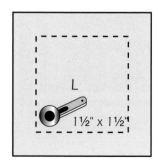

L

1½" x 1½"

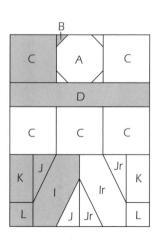

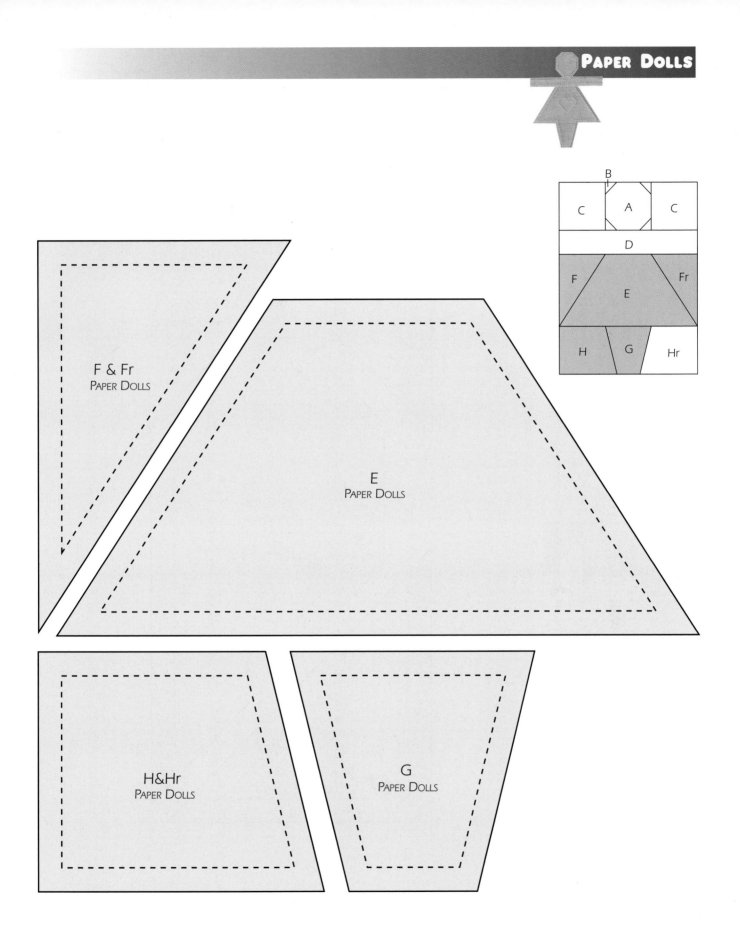

F & Fr
PAPER DOLLS

E
PAPER DOLLS

H&Hr
PAPER DOLLS

G
PAPER DOLLS

B
C   A   C
D
F   E   Fr
H   G   Hr

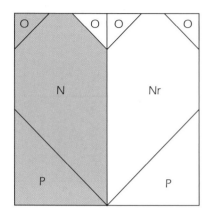

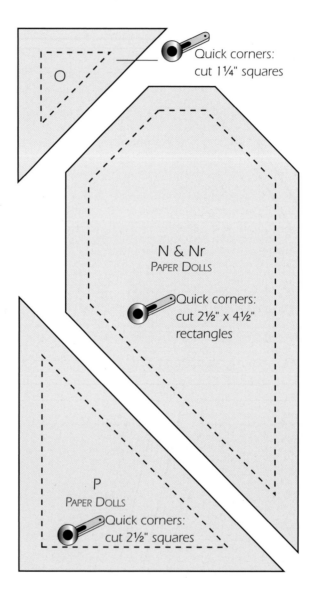

Quick corners:
cut 1¼" squares

N & Nr
PAPER DOLLS

Quick corners:
cut 2½" x 4½"
rectangles

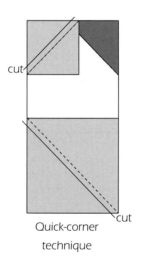

cut

cut

Quick-corner
technique

P
PAPER DOLLS

Quick corners:
cut 2½" squares

WE'RE HAVING A TEA PARTY

My daughter likes to have tea parties with her friends and dolls. This quilt is one of her favorites, and I'm sure it will be a delight to other little girls as well. Your child might like to help you choose colors for the teacups.

WE'RE HAVING A TEA PARTY, hand quilted by Leesa Loyd

Cutting Instructions

Quilt 40" x 48"

11 teacup blocks, 8" x 8", 3 teapot blocks, 8" x 8"

17 flower blocks, 4" x 4"

Fabrics	Yards	Patches
Scraps	—	
teacups		11 C1, 11 C3, 11 C7
teapot 1		1 T1, 1 T4, 1 T4r, 1 T6, 1 T7, 1 T 9, 1 T10
teapot 2		1 T2, 1 T6, 1 T20,1 T25, 1T26, 1 T27, 1 T31
teapot 3		1 T2, 1 T6, 1 T13, 1 T15, 1 T16, 1 T18 1 T20, 1 T21, 1 T24
Pink	¼	
flower center		68 F1
Yellow	⅝	
flower petals		68 F4, 68 F5
Green	½	
leaves		68 F8, 68 F9
Blue	¾	
flower background		68 F2, 68 F3, 68 F6 68 F7, 136 F10
Background	1¼	
		22 C2, 11 C3, 11 C3r, 11 C4, 11 C5, 11 C6 11 C8, 11 C9, 12 F11, 13 T2, 5 T3, 1 T4, 1 T4r, 5 T5, 3 T6, 1 T7, 2 T8 1 T9, 2 T10, 1 T11 2 T12, 1 T14, 2 T16 1 T17, 1 T19,1 T20, 1 T22, 1 T23, 1 T25, 1 T28, 2 T29, 1 T30
Inner border (mitered)	⅜	5 strips 1½" selvage to selvage
Outer border (mitered)	⅝	5 strips 3½" selvage to selvage
Backing	2⅝	2 panels 26½" x 44"
Binding (optional)	½	2½" x 5¼ yds.
Batting		44" x 52"

CUTTING PATCHES

The Cutting Instructions show the number of patches to cut for each fabric.

SCISSOR CUTTING

Use the patterns on pages 72-76 to make templates for the patches listed in the Cutting Instructions. Skip to Piecing Blocks.

ROTARY CUTTING

Rotary cutting dimensions are given in the patterns. Look for the rotary cutter symbol. You will need templates for patterns that do not have the rotary symbol.

PIECING BLOCKS

FLOWERS

The flower units can be made by add-a-strip piecing, page 10. This method is frequently used by machine piecers to make Log Cabin blocks.

Cut strips the widths given on the pattern pieces. Sew a pink F1 strip to a blue F2 strip to make a band. Slice the band into 1½" sections (Fig. 1).

Sew the sections to a second blue F3 strip as shown in Fig. 2. Cut the pieces apart and press.

Sew these pieces to the F4 strip, then cut and press as before. Following the number sequence in the pattern, continue to add strips to the units until you have completed 68 partial flower units (Fig. 3).

Make a flower template (pattern on page 76) from see-through plastic and use it to trim the partial flower units to size, as follows: Lay the template on the unit, aligning it with the flower as shown in Fig. 4.

Cut off the triangles on both sides of the template.

Attach the F10 triangles to the edges just trimmed to complete the flower unit (Fig. 5). Make 68 units.

Sew 4 flower units together to make a 4" (finished) small flower block. Make 17 small flower blocks.

Sew a 4½" background square (F11) to each of 12 small flower blocks (Fig. 6). Then use these to make 6 large flower blocks (see page 71). Keep the remaining 5 small blocks to use in the border.

TEA CUPS AND POTS

Follow the Block Assembly diagrams to make 11 teacups and one of each of the 3 teapots.

ASSEMBLING QUILT

Place the completed blocks in order on a flat surface, as shown in the Quilt Assembly diagram (page 71). Sew the blocks in rows across the quilt, then sew the rows together.

ADDING BORDERS

Notice that 3 of the border corners are mitered. The lower-left corner has a flower block, however, which will be sewn to the quilt with the partial-seam technique.

To make the border sections, sew an inner border strip to each outer border strip. There will be a total of 5 of these combined strips. Cut the following lengths from the combined strips. (Label the border strips A–E as you cut them.

3 A sections	10½" long
1 B sections	30½"
1 C sections	38½"
2 D sections	26½"
1 E sections	18½"

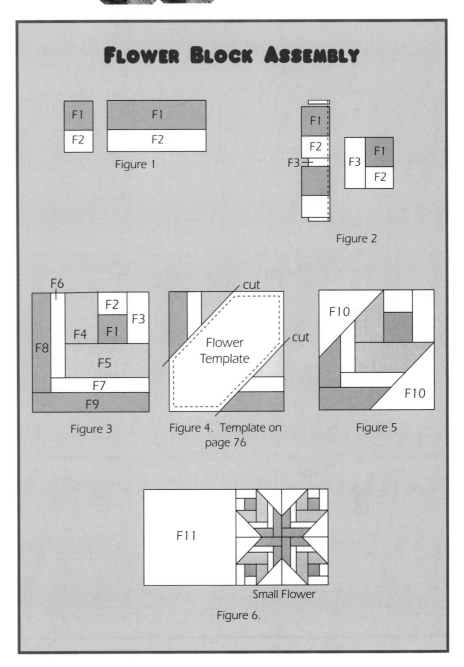

FLOWER BLOCK ASSEMBLY

Figure 1

Figure 2

Figure 3

Figure 4. Template on page 76

Figure 5

Figure 6.

Small Flower

Referring to the Quilt Assembly diagram, sew the appropriate border sections on either side of 4 of the flower blocks to make the top, bottom, and 2 side borders. At this point, the border strips are longer than needed, but they will be trimmed after the corners are mitered. Align the flower blocks with the appropriate quilt blocks and pin all 4 borders to the quilt top. Reserve one block for the corner.

Note: The left border will be sewn all the way to the bottom edge of the quilt, but for the bottom border, leave at least 6" unsewn at the lower-left corner.

BORDER: LOWER-LEFT CORNER

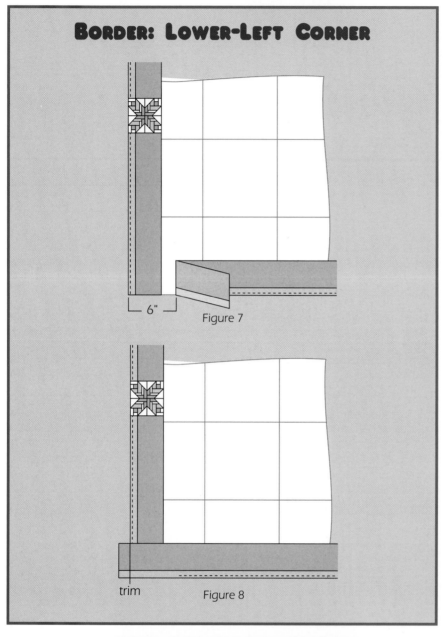

6"

Figure 7

trim   Figure 8

Sew all the borders to the quilt, starting and stopping the stitching lines ¼" in from the corners that will be mitered. Sew the 3 miters and trim off the extra fabric (at the miters only), leaving ¼" seam allowances.

Fold the bottom border out of the way and trim the left side border even with the quilt edge (Fig. 7). Do not press the border open, yet.

Place the bottom border on top of the side border and trim off the extra length even with the raw edge of the quilt (Fig. 8). Press the left border outward.

Sew the last small flower block to the end of the bottom border and press the block outward. Finish sewing the bottom border to the quilt.

FINISHING

Finish the quilt the quick-turn way. Then quilt as desired. Or, you can quilt the layers and finish the raw edges with binding.

QUILTING IDEAS

1. Quilt a small design inside each teacup and teapot.
2. Emphasize the pots and cups by quilting around each one, either in the ditch or ¼" outside them.
3. Quilt a diagonal grid in the back ground.
4. A 2"–2½" border design will fit nicely in the outer border.

Need Help?

Add-a-strip piecing	p. 10
Chain piecing	p. 10
Mitered corner	p. 13
Quick corner	p. 11
Quick-turn finishing	p. 15
Rotary cutting	p. 8
Templates	p. 8

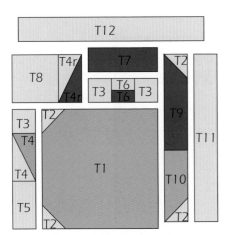

Teapot 1 Block Assembly

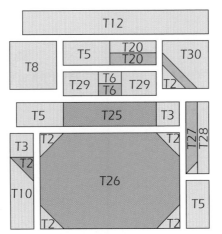

Teapot 2 Block Assembly

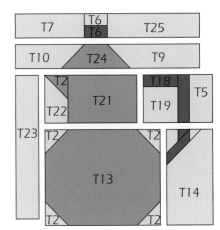

Teapot 3 Block Assembly

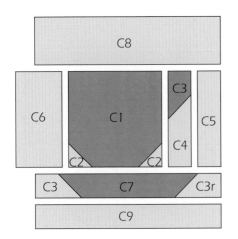

Teacup Block Assembly

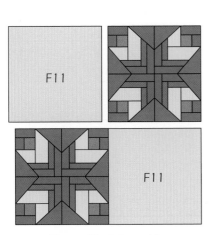

Flower Block Assembly

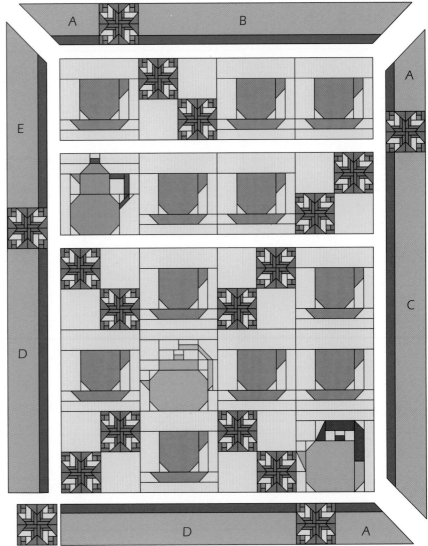

Quilt Assembly

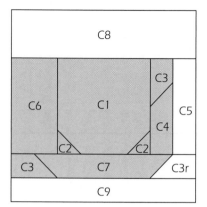

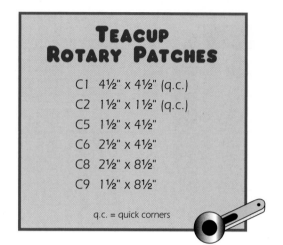

TEACUP ROTARY PATCHES

C1 4½" x 4½" (q.c.)

C2 1½" x 1½" (q.c.)

C5 1½" x 4½"

C6 2½" x 4½"

C8 2½" x 8½"

C9 1½" x 8½"

q.c. = quick corners

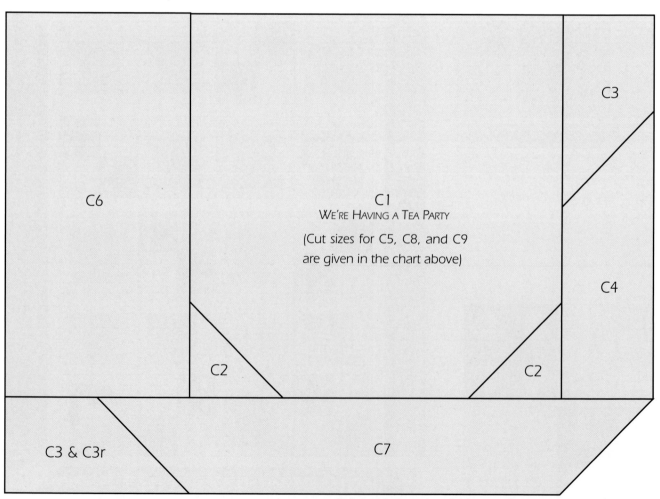

C6

C3

C1

WE'RE HAVING A TEA PARTY

(Cut sizes for C5, C8, and C9
are given in the chart above)

C4

C2

C2

C3 & C3r

C7

Full-size block section. Add seam allowances.

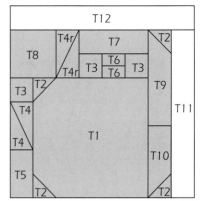

TEAPOT 1 ROTARY PATCHES

T1	5½" x 5½" (q.c.)	T8	2½" x 2½"
T2	1½" x 1½" (q.c.)	T9	1½" x 4 ½" (q.c.)
T3	1½" x 1½"	T10	1½" x 3½" (q.c.)
T5	½" x 2½"	T11	1½" x 7½"
T6	1" x 1½"	T12	1½" x 8½"
T7	1½" x 3½"		q.c. = quick corners

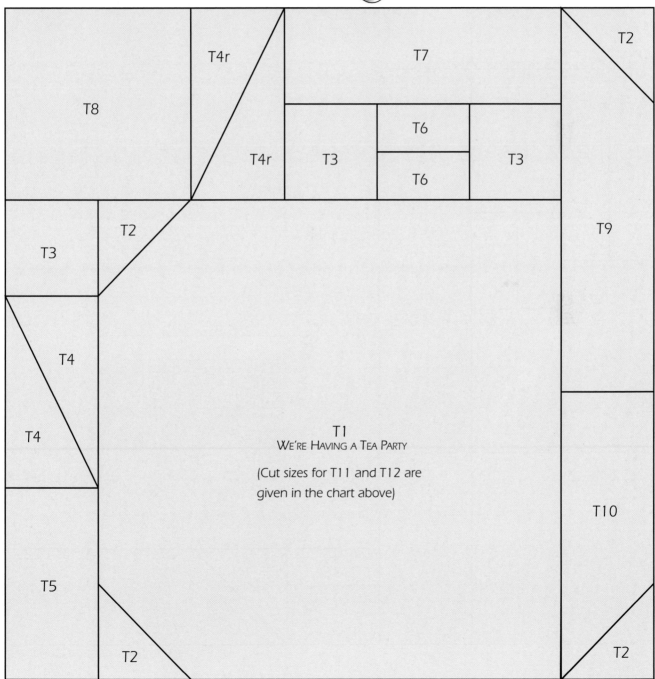

T1
WE'RE HAVING A TEA PARTY

(Cut sizes for T11 and T12 are
given in the chart above)

Full-size block section. Add seam allowances.

TEAPOT 2

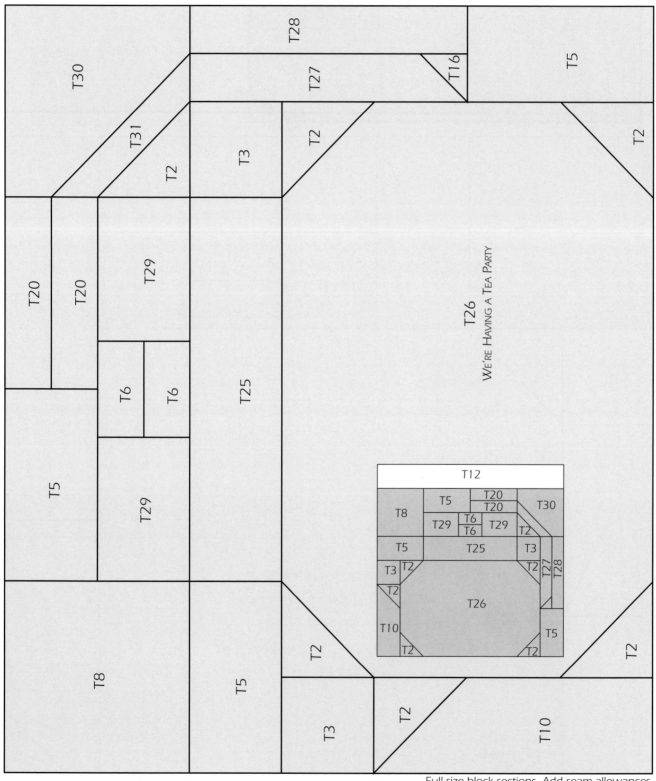

Full-size block sections. Add seam allowances.

TEAPOT 3

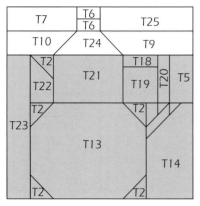

(Top section of teapot on page 76.)

ROTARY PATCHES FOR TEAPOTS 2 & 3

T12 1½" x 8½"	T22 1½" x 2½" (q.c.)
T13 4½" x 5½" (q.c.)	T23 1½" x 6½"
T16 1⅜" x 1⅜"	T25 1½" x 4½"
T18 1" x 2"	T26 4½" x 6½" (q.c.)
T19 2" x 2"	T28 1" x 3½"
T20 1" x 2½"	T29 1½" x 2"
T21 1½" x 3½"	

q.c. = quick corners

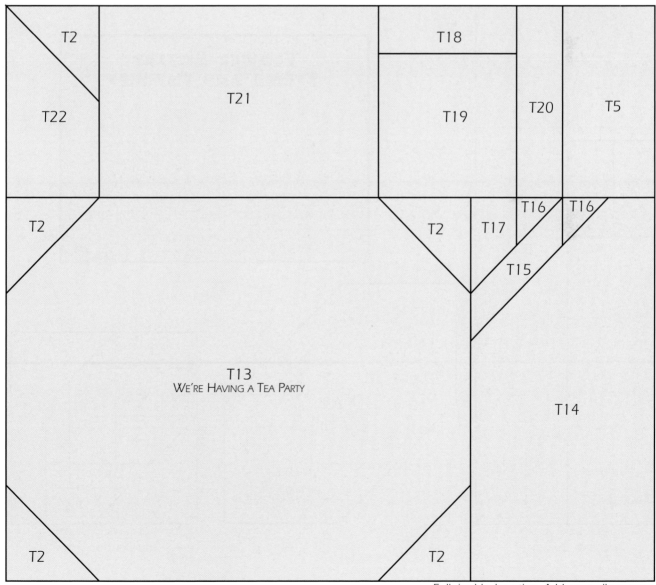

Full-size block section. Add seam allowances.

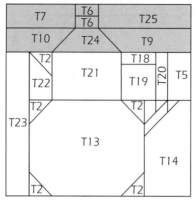

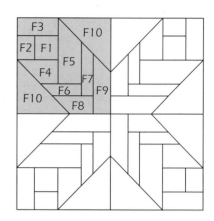

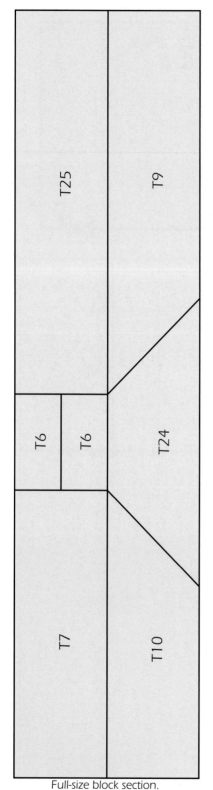

FLOWER ROTARY STRIPS AND PATCHES

F1 1" (a.p.)   F7 ¾" (a.p.)
F2 ⅞" (a.p.)   F8 ⅞" (a.p.)
F3 ⅞" (a.p.)   F9 ⅞" (a.p.)
F4 1" (a.p.)   F10 2" x 2" (h.s.)
F5 1" (a.p.)   F11 4½" x 4½"
F6 ¾" (a.p.)

a.p. = add-a-strip piecing
h.s. = half-square triangles

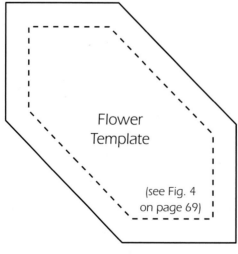

Flower Template

(see Fig. 4 on page 69)

Full-size block section.
Add seam allowances.

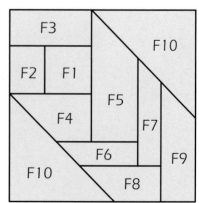

Full-size block section.
Add seam allowances.

LET'S SAIL AWAY

This quilt is guaranteed to be full of fun for your youngster, and it will be fun to make as well. It is filled with surprises at every turn. The children will get plenty of practice with buttons, by opening and closing the front sails on these colorful sailboats.

Buttons are NOT recommended for infants or small children because buttons may present a choking hazard.

LET'S SAIL AWAY, hand quilting by Leesa Lloyd

CUTTING INSTRUCTIONS

Quilt 48" x 56"

15 sailboat blocks, 6" x 6"

FABRICS	YARDS	PATCHES
Novelty Print Scraps	—	
hidden pieces (under flap)		15 B
Scraps	—	
back sails		15 A
front sails (flaps)		15 B
Red, Green, Navy	⅛ each	
hulls		5 D each, 5 F each
White	1⅝	
hull stripe		15 E
background		15 A, 15 C, 15 G, 15 H
flap linings		15 Br
checkerboard		71 I
Dark blue	¾	
checkerboard		117 I
Light blue	1⅛	
checkerboard		202 I
Border (butted)	⅔	2 strips 3½" x 58½"
		2 strips 3½" x 50½"
Backing	3⅛	2 panels 30½" x 52"
Binding (optional)	1½	2½" x 6⅛ yds.
Batting		52" x 60"

Supplies

Buttons: 15 size ½" in assorted colors

Elastic: ⅛" x 24"

CUTTING PATCHES

The fabrics used for the sail flaps and the flap linings should be prewashed to prevent the sails from shrinking when the quilt is washed.

The Cutting Instructions show the number of patches to cut for each fabric.

SCISSOR CUTTING

Use the patterns on pages 83-84 to make templates for the pieces listed in the Cutting Instructions. Skip to Piecing Blocks.

ROTARY CUTTING

Rotary cutting dimensions are given in the patterns. Look for the rotary cutter symbol. The boat hulls and the checkerboard background can be strip pieced, and the G and H patches can be quick pieced from squares by using the quick-corner method (see Quick Piecing, page 9). You will need templates for patterns that do not have the rotary cutter symbol.

PIECING BLOCKS

Following the Block Assembly diagram, page 84, make 15 sailboat hulls. For rotary cutting instructions see page 80 under Quick Piecing.

To make the front sail flaps, cut 15 pieces of elastic 1½" long. Place a piece of elastic on a white Br patch, right side up, as shown in Figure 1. Measure up from the bottom ⅜", and sew the elastic loop in place ⅛" in from the edge.

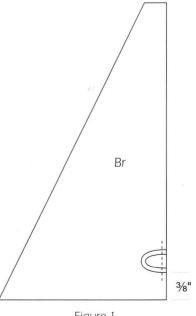

Figure 1

Place a scrap B on a white Br, right sides together (with the elastic loop on the inside). With a ¼" seam allowance, stitch down the long edge, across the elastic, to the bottom of the patch. Without removing the needle, turn the piece around and, in the seam allowance, stitch back through the elastic. Turn the piece again and stitch through the elastic for a third time. (This extra stitching will help prevent the elastic from being pulled out during use.) Stop, with the needle down, ¼" from the bottom edge.

Turn the piece and sew across the bottom with a ¼" seam allowance (Fig. 2). Trim seam allowance at the point if needed, turn the sail flap right side out, and press. To complete the sail flap, top stitch ⅛" in from the edge on the side and bottom (Fig. 3). Repeat to make 15 sail flaps.

Align a sail flap, right side up, on top of a novelty print B patch, also right side up, as shown in Figure 4. (The elastic loop will be on the left. The top right corners should be aligned, and there will be approximately ¼" of the novelty fabric showing on the left and bottom edges.) Staystitch the two pieces together ⅛" in from the right edge.

Sew a background C patch to a sail flap with a ¼" seam allowance (Fig. 5). Press this unit with the sail flap open to the right so the seam allowance can be pressed toward the novelty print (Fig. 6). This step is important because it will give the sail flap a rounded, full-sail look when it is buttoned. Repeat these steps to make 15 front-sail units.

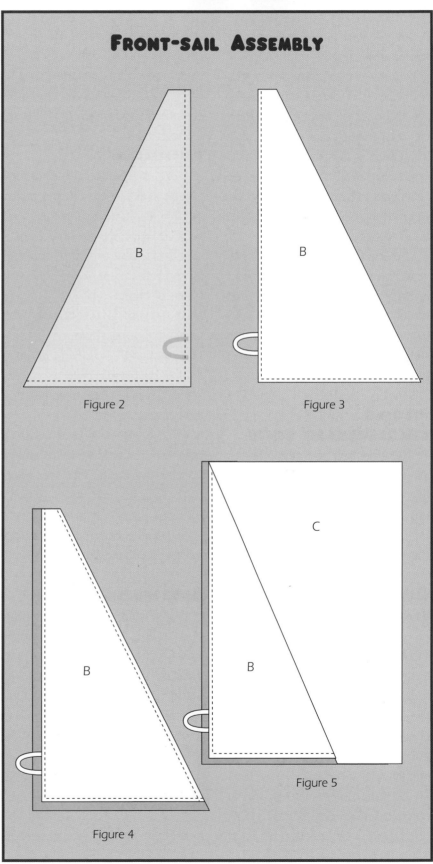

FRONT-SAIL ASSEMBLY

Figure 2

Figure 3

Figure 4

Figure 5

Make 15 back-sail units using the A patches. Stack all the boat units, in sewing order, resembling the block. If you want to coordinate front- sails with back sails, decide which pieces are to go together before stacking them (see block diagram on page 83). Sew the front-sail and back-sail units together at the center seam. Be careful not to catch the sail flap in the seam. Press the center seam allowances toward the back-sail units.

To attach the sails to a boat hull, leave the sail flap open while stitching. The seam comes very close to the bottom edge of the flap, so leaving it open will help prevent a curved seam. Complete the sewing of all 15 boat blocks.

PIECING CHECKERBOARD UNITS

Whether you are using individually cut patches or strip-pieced slices (see Checkerboard under Quick Piecing below), make the number of checkerboard units shown in the Unit Assembly diagrams on page 82.

QUICK PIECING
BOAT HULL UNITS

Following the rotary measurements on the patch patterns, cut D, E, and F strips. Sew the strips together to make a band for each of the three boat colors, as shown in Fig. 7. Press seam allowances away from the center strip. Cut each band into five 6½" sections.

To quick piece the G and H patches, cut 15 G (1⅜") and 15 H (2") squares. On the back of each square, mark a pencil line from corner to corner. Position the squares on the boat hulls, right sides together. Sew along the pencil line and cut off the extra fabric, leaving a ¼" seam allowance (Fig. 8). Press the triangles open.

CHECKERBOARD

The checkerboard background can be strip pieced. Cut the following 2½"-wide strips, selvage to selvage: 6 white, 16 light blue, and 9 dark blue. Sew the strips together length-wise to make the following bands of strips:
Make 2, band 1 – dk. blue, lt. blue, white, lt. blue, dk. blue.
Make 2, band 2 – lt. blue, dk. blue, lt. blue, dk. blue, lt. blue.
Make 1, band 3 – white, lt. blue, dk. blue, lt. blue, white.
Make 2, band 4 – lt. blue, white, lt. blue.

Cut the bands into 2½" slices (A–D). To make the E slices, remove a dark blue patch from one end of 6 A slices. Sew the slices together to make the block units shown on page 82.

ASSEMBLING QUILT

Now that all the units have been made, the quilt top can be sewn together. On a flat surface, arrange the blocks and checkerboard units, as shown in the Quilt Assembly diagram. Sew the units in rows across the quilt, then sew the rows together.

ADDING BORDERS

Cut 6 3½" strips across the dark blue fabric, from selvage to selvage. Splice the strips as needed to create the lengths given in the Cutting Instructions. Sew the borders to the quilt top and miter the corners.

FINISHING

After the quilt is layered and quilted, use heavy thread to sew the buttons on each of the sailboats. (Use the X marked on template A as a placement guide.) Be sure to sew the buttons securely, since this quilt will be used by children. The elastic should just fit around the buttons, without being stretched. The sail flap should lie flat and smooth.

QUILTING IDEAS

1. To emphasize the diagonal pattern, you can quilt diagonally through all the dark and light blue squares.
2. Quilt free-form waves under each sailboat.
3. Stitch in the ditch around each sailboat, or echo quilt ¼" away from each one.
4. A 2½"–2¾" wide quilting design will fit nicely in the border.

Need Help?	
Butted corners	p. 13
Chain piecing	p. 10
Quick corner	p. 11
Quick-turn finishing	p. 15
Rotary cutting	p. 8
Strip piecing	p. 10
Templates	p. 8

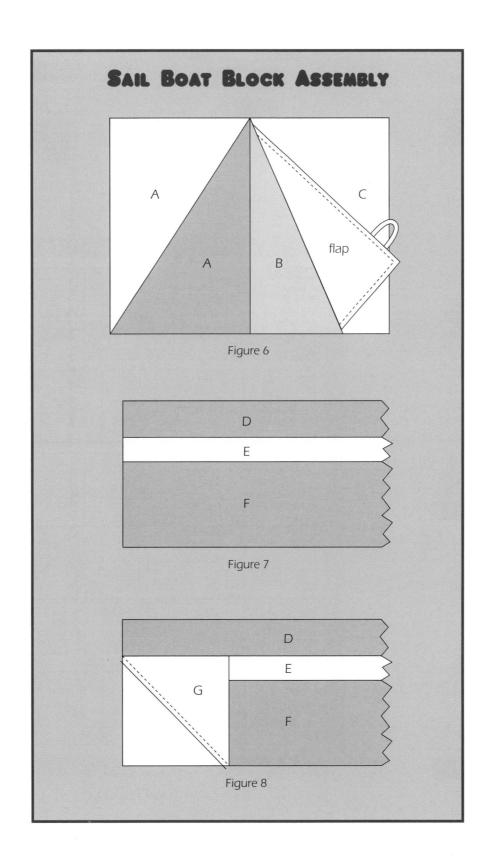

SAIL BOAT BLOCK ASSEMBLY

Figure 6

Figure 7

Figure 8

Cut slices from bands of strips.

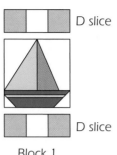

D slice

D slice

Block 1
(make 2)

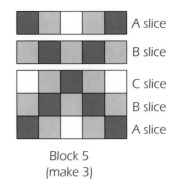

A slice

B slice

C slice

B slice

A slice

Block 5
(make 3)

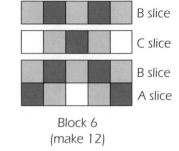

B slice

C slice

B slice

A slice

Block 6
(make 12)

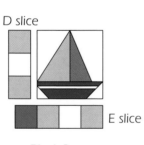

D slice

Block 2
(make 7)

D slice

E slice

Block 3
(make 3)

D slice

E slice

Block 4
(make 3)

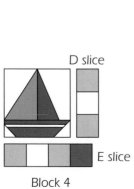

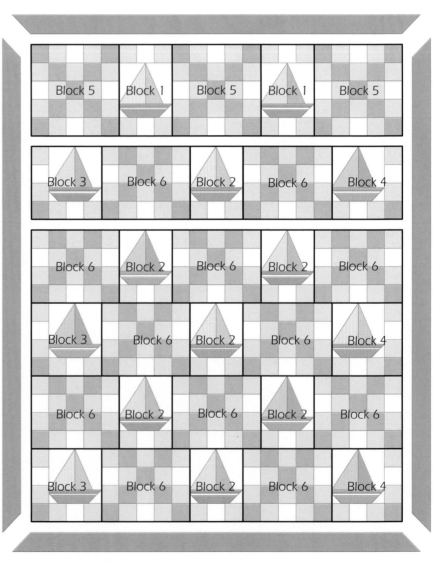

Block 5	Block 1	Block 5	Block 1	Block 5
Block 3	Block 6	Block 2	Block 6	Block 4
Block 6	Block 2	Block 6	Block 2	Block 6
Block 3	Block 6	Block 2	Block 6	Block 4
Block 6	Block 2	Block 6	Block 2	Block 6
Block 3	Block 6	Block 2	Block 6	Block 4

Quilt Assembly

STITCH A CHILD'S QUILT, Vicki M. A. Thomas

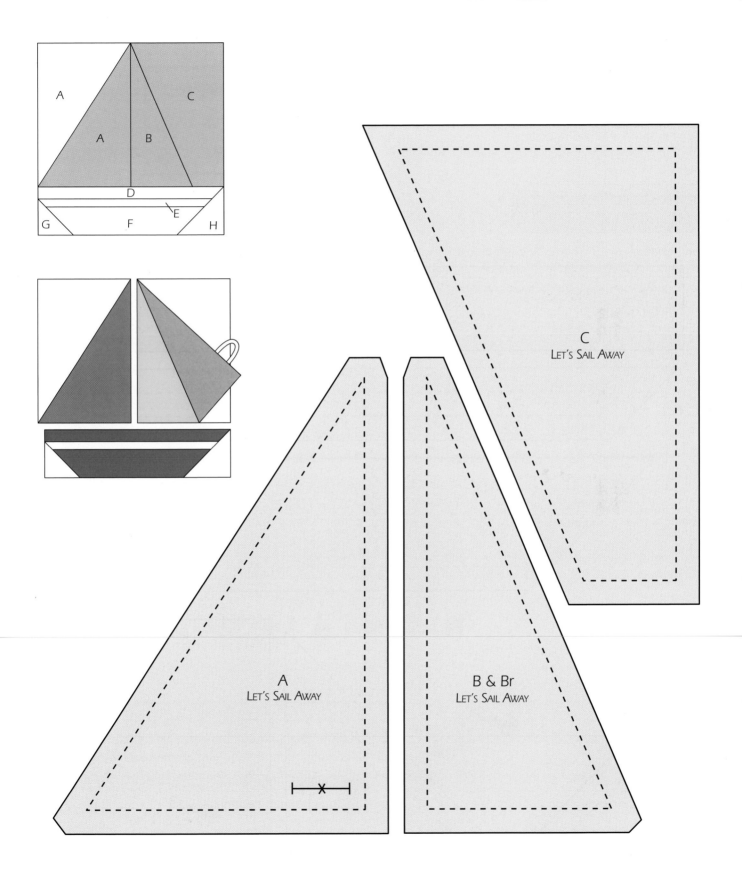

A
LET'S SAIL AWAY

B & Br
LET'S SAIL AWAY

C
LET'S SAIL AWAY

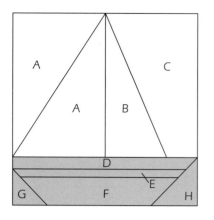

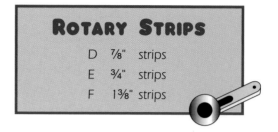

ROTARY STRIPS

D ⅞" strips
E ¾" strips
F 1⅜" strips

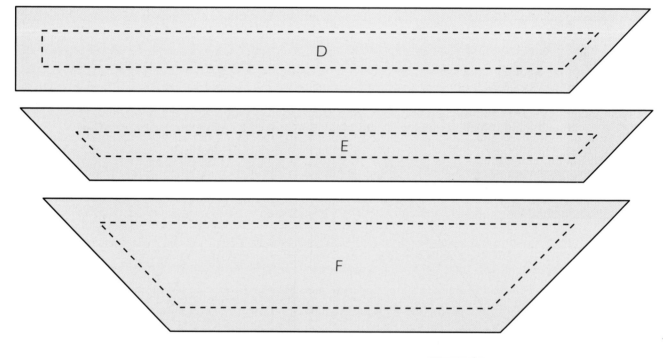

D

E

F

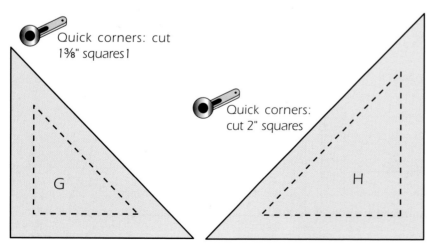

Quick corners: cut
1⅜" squares1

G

Quick corners:
cut 2" squares

H

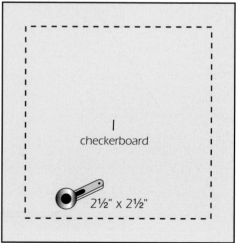

I
checkerboard

2½" x 2½"

Up Up and Away

I have always dreamed of flying in a hot-air balloon. Wouldn't it be wonderful! Just imagine the sights from that high in the air. I love all the beautiful colors and designs and the way the balloons gracefully drift across the sky.

Up, Up and Away

CUTTING INSTRUCTIONS
Quilt 46" x 56"
14 balloon blocks, 10" x 10"

Fabrics	Yards	Patches
Scraps (balloons)	—	14 A, 14 D, 14 G 14 I, 14 J
Background (balloons)	1¾	14 B, 14 Br, 14 C, 28 E, 28 F, 28 H, 28 K, 28 L, 14 M, 6 N
Border (butted)	¾	2 strips 3½" x 52½" 2 strips 3½" x 48½"
Backing	3	2 panels 30½ " x 50"
Binding (optional)	½	2½" x 6 yds.
Batting		50" x 60"

CUTTING PATCHES

The full-size patterns given on pages 88-89 are for Balloon Block 1. There are 3 variations given for the I patch, which are presented as full-size block sections (pages 90–91). To make patterns from the block sections, trace each patch on template material. Be sure to add ¼" seam allowances.

To design your own patterns for the G and I patches, trace the G or I patch outline on paper and draw the desired pattern inside the outline. Then proceed as described for a block section.

SCISSOR CUTTING

Use the balloon patterns to make templates for the patches listed in the Cutting Instructions. Skip to Piecing Blocks.

ROTARY CUTTING

Rotary cutting dimensions are given in the patterns. Look for the rotary cutter symbol. For the half-square triangles, cut a square the size given, then cut the square in half diagonally to make 2 half-square triangles. You will need templates for patterns that do not have the rotary symbol.

PIECING BLOCKS

The balloons can be pieced in 3 sections (see Block Assembly diagram, page 88). Make 14 of each section. Sew sections 1, 2, and 3 together for each block, then add the remaining L and M patches as shown.

ASSEMBLING QUILT

Lay the completed balloons and the solid blocks (N pieces) on a flat surface in the positions you think look best. Set the blocks in 5 rows with 4 blocks in each row. Sew the blocks in rows across the quilt, then sew the rows together.

ADDING BORDERS

Cut five 3½" strips for the borders (selvage to selvage) and splice them as needed to make the lengths given in the Cutting Instructions. Sew the two longest strips to the sides of the quilt and trim off any extra length even with the quilt's edges. Then sew the remaining strips to the top and bottom and trim as before.

FINISHING

Use the quick-turn method for layering the quilt and finishing the edges, if you like, then quilt as desired. Or, you can use traditional methods for layering and binding your quilt.

QUILTING IDEAS

1. Stitch in the ditch or outline stitch around each balloon and the border.
2. Use an over-all design or grid design in the background. Straight stitch lines or small designs in the balloons.
3. Use a 2" to 2½" design in the border.
4. Embroider or machine stitch basket ropes with colored thread.

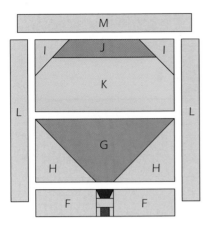

Block 1 Assembly

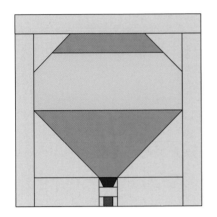

Completed Block 1

Quilt Assembly

Need Help?

Butted corners	p. 13
Chain piecing	p. 10
Quick-turn finishing	p. 15
Rotary cutting	p. 8
Splicing strips	p. 12
Templates	p. 8

BASIC BALLOON

SECTION 1

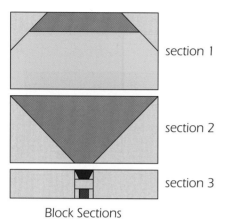

section 1

section 2

section 3

Block Sections

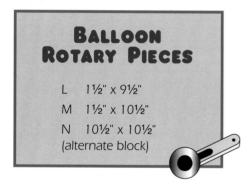

BALLOON ROTARY PIECES

L   1½" x 9½"

M 1½" x 10½"

N 10½" x 10½"
(alternate block)

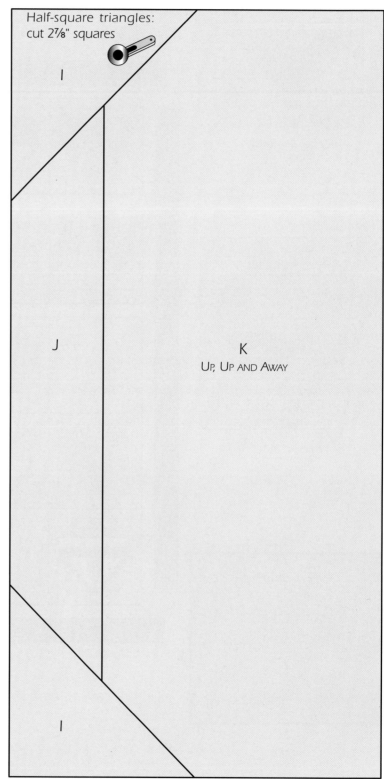

Half-square triangles:
cut 2⅞" squares

I

J

K
Up, Up and Away

I

Full-size block sections. Add seam allowances.

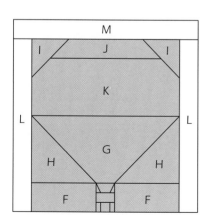

M

I   J   I

K

L   L

G

H   H

F   F

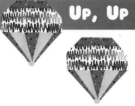

SECTION 2

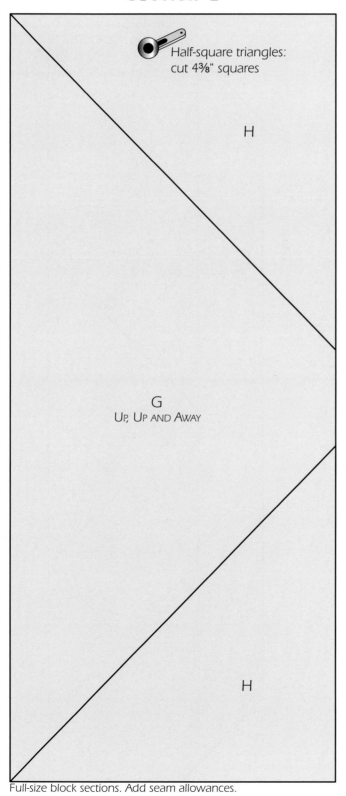

Half-square triangles:
cut 4⅜" squares

H

G
Up, Up and Away

H

Full-size block sections. Add seam allowances.

SECTION 3

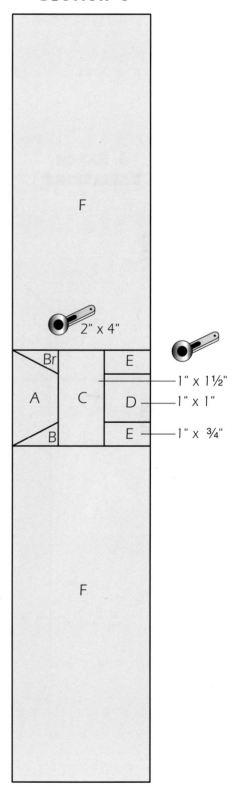

F

2" x 4"

Br

A C E

1" x 1½"

D

1" x 1"

B E

1" x ¾"

F

BALLOON VARIATIONS

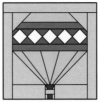

K PATCH VARIATION

J PATCH VARIATIONS

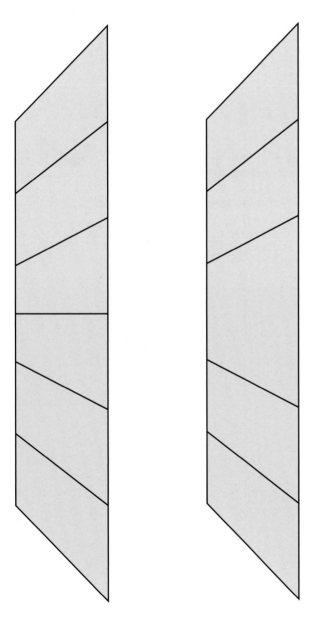

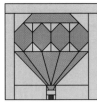

K Patch
Variations Continued

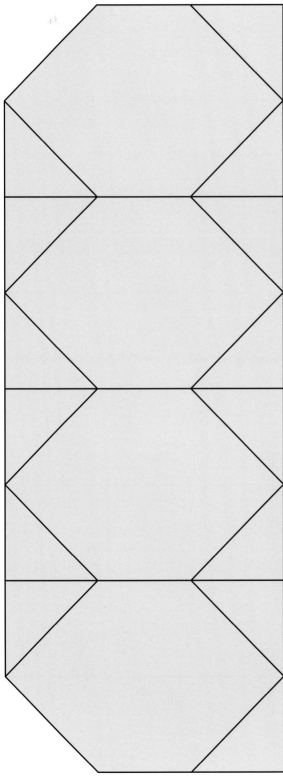

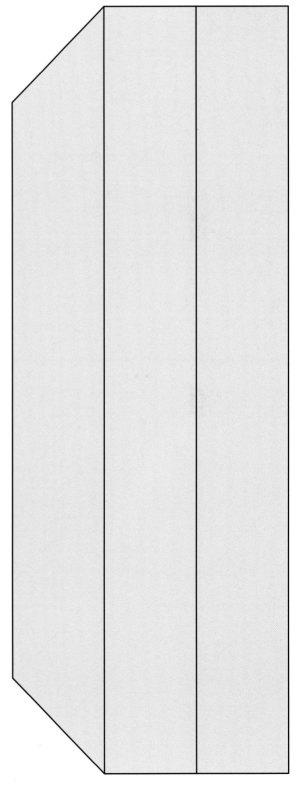

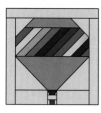

K Patch
Variations Continued

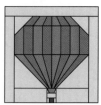

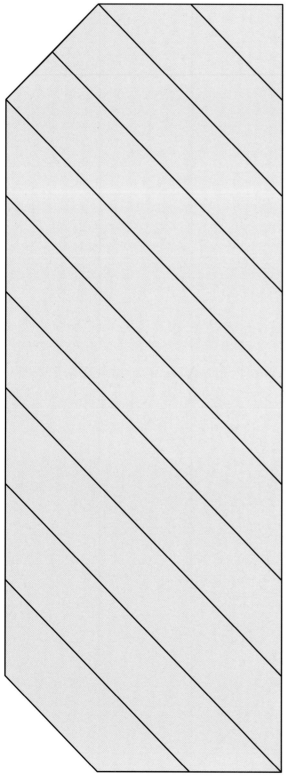

G Patch Variations

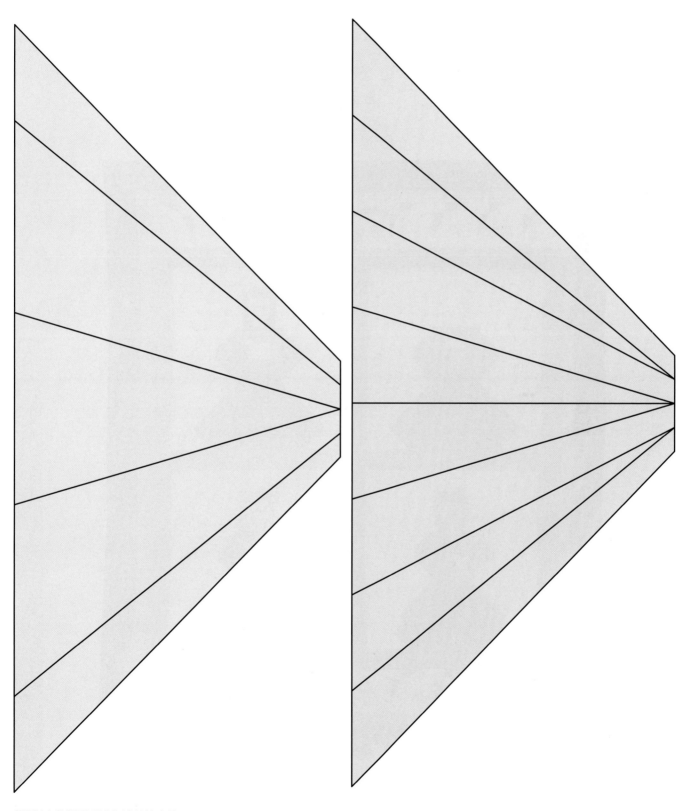

I Believe In Angels

This pattern was created during a period of reflective silence, and it was truly a gift from Heaven. It reminds me that all children are different and most precious and that their innocence needs guidance, love, and protection by everyone. Children are all beautiful, no matter where in the world they live. They are the world's Littlest Angels.

I BELIEVE IN ANGELS

For those who like foundation piecing, portions of the angel faces and upper bodies can be paper pieced. Just copy the full-size patterns and cut them into logical sewing units. Remember to leave ¼" seam allowances around the outside edges of the paper-pieced sections. Then sew the sections together, matching seams as usual.

CUTTING PATCHES

Pre-wash face fabric to remove chemicals so the paint will adhere better.

Each of the angels is slightly different. There are 4 angel heads and 4 upper bodies. You can make all 4 angels alike, or you can mix and match.

The patterns for the angels are given as full-size block sections (pages 99-104). To make templates from the block sections, trace each patch on template material. Be sure to add ¼" seam allowances.

In addition, there are two different skirts, which are given together in the full-size pattern on page 101. Notice that the bottom half of the harp is also provided in this pattern section.

Because there are so many pieces to the angel quilt, you may want to cut only what you need at any one time. You can keep the patches in labeled, zippered plastic bags.

CUTTING INSTRUCTIONS

Quilt 46" x 54"
4 angel blocks, 16" x 16"; 16 flower blocks, 4" x 4"
1 double flower block, 4" x 6"
1 bow block, 4" x 6"

FABRICS	YARDS	PATCHES
Scraps	—	faces, necks, hands, hair, halos, book, harp, and dove
dresses	⅜ each	1 each (see photo, pg. 94)
wings	⅝	various patches in the head, upper body, and skirt sections
Flowers and Bow		
dark pink (centers)	⅛	18 F1
light pink (bow and petals)	¼	2 B1, 2 B2, 2 B3, 18 F1, 18 F3, 18 F3r
green (leaves)	⅛	16 F3, 16 F3r, 1 F5, 1F5r, 2 F6
Background	¾	
angels		4 A, 8 B, 24 C, 4 D, 4 Dr, 8 E, 8 F
flowers & bow	½	66 F1, 18 F2, 34 F3, 34 F3r, 2 F4, 2 F7, 2 B4
Sashes	½	3 strips 2½" x 40½" 6 strips 2½" x 18½"
Border 1 (butted)	⅜	2 strips 1½" x 48½" 2 strips 1½" x 42½"
Border 2 (butted)	⅝	2 strips 3½" x 50½" 2 strips 3½" x 48½"
Backing	3	2 panels 29½" x 50"
Binding	⅝	2½" x 5⅞ yds.
Batting		50" x 58"

Supplies
paint pen or fine-point permanent marker for eyelashes
fabric paint for cheeks, Stencil brush, size 1, 2, or 3, Wax paper

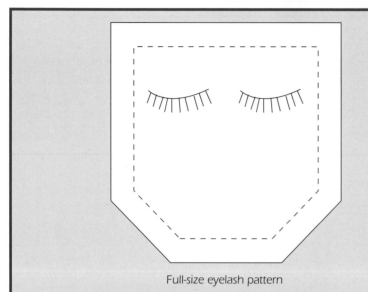

Full-size eyelash pattern

PAINTING THE ANGEL FACE

Use the following method to paint the cheeks with a dry stencil brush and pink fabric paint:

Do not use water, which will cause the paint to smear. Squeeze a small amount of paint on a paper plate. Tap the brush in the paint and then tap the brush on the paper plate to remove the excess. The tips of the bristles should have only a small amount of paint on them. You can practice on the paper plate. Gently tap the bristles of the brush on the fabric, depositing small amounts of paint each time. Apply only the amount of paint needed to highlight the cheeks. Use the paint pen to draw eyelashes. Allow the paint to dry before sewing the units.

SCISSOR CUTTING

Use the block sections on pages 99–106 to make templates. Skip to Piecing Angel Blocks.

ROTARY CUTTING

Rotary cutting dimensions are given in the patterns. Look for the rotary cutter symbol. You will need templates for patterns that do not have the rotary symbol.

PIECING ANGEL BLOCKS

The skirt pattern and the lower part of the wings and sleeves are on page 101. Make a skirt section for each angel.

The main wing sections on page 98 are the same for all the angel blocks. Press the seam allowances toward the wing pieces. Make 4 left and 4 right wing sections.

The upper body sections are different for each angel. One angel is praying, one holds a book, another holds a dove, and one is playing the harp. Make an upper body section for each angel.

There are 4 different head sections. Make 1 for each angel.

The faces should be painted before the sections are sewn together. Use the eyelash pattern above to

paint eyelashes for each angel. Practice on a scrap of fabric first. Then place the faces on wax paper and draw the eyelashes.

Use the block sections and the patches to make the angel blocks, as shown in the Block Assembly diagrams given with each pattern.

PIECING FLOWER BLOCKS

A portion of the flower can be strip pieced, if you like. Sew a 1½"-wide pink strip (F1, flower centers) to a 1½" background strip (F1 patches) to make a band. Then cut 18 pieces, 1½" wide, from the band.

Use add-a-strip piecing (page 12) to sew these pieces to another 1½"-wide background strip. Press the pieces away from the strip and cut the new units apart. Following the Block Assembly diagrams on pages 103 and 104, make 16 flower blocks and 1 double flower block.

PIECING BOW BLOCK

Pieces B1, B2, and B3 are double thicknesses. For the center of the bow (piece B1), cut 2 pieces 1½" x 2". With right sides together, sew both the 2 long sides together with a ¼" seam allowance to make a tube (Fig. 1). Turn the tube right side out and press. It should measure 1" x 2".

For the top portion of the bow (piece B2), cut 2 pieces 2½" x 8" and sew them, right sides together, down both 8" sides to make a tube. Turn this piece right side out and press.

For the bottom portion (piece B3), cut two pieces 1½" x 10" and

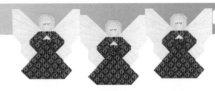
sew them together as before on both of the 10" sides. Turn and press.

Use the following method to sew the B1 piece and the 2 background B4 pieces together: Fold each B4 piece in half crosswise and finger crease the fold to mark the center. Find and mark the center of the B1 piece, also. Matching centers, place the B1 piece in between the B4 pieces (right sides together) as shown in Fig. 2. Sew all three pieces together and press the unit open (Fig. 3).

Find and mark the centers of pieces B2 and B3. Thread both pieces through the B1 loop and center them inside the loop. Position the B2 piece ends in the upper corners, ¼" down from the top edge, and pin in place. Let the extra length extend beyond the edges of the block. Position the B3 ends so that they cover the bottom corners; pin in place.

When the bow looks the way you want, staystitch the pieces ⅛" from the edges of the block. Trim B2 and B3 even with the edges of the block (Fig.4).

BOW ROTARY PATCHES

B1   1½" x 2"
B2   2½" x 8"
B3   1½" x 10"
B4   2½" x 6½"

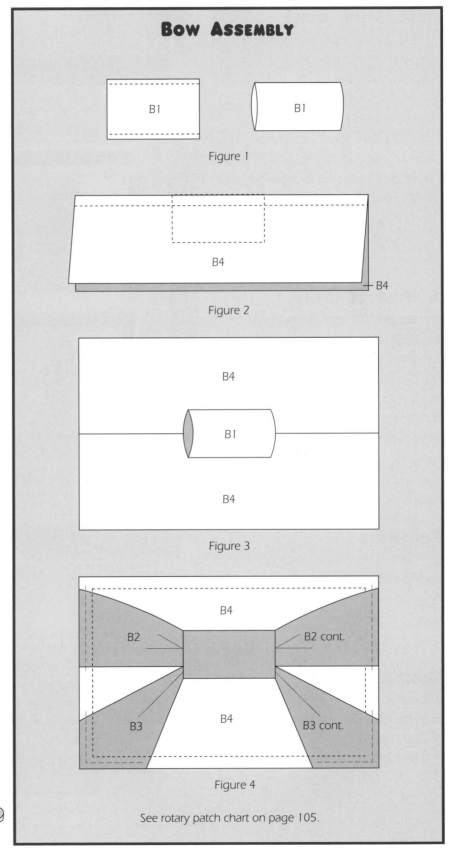

BOW ASSEMBLY

Figure 1

Figure 2

Figure 3

Figure 4

See rotary patch chart on page 105.

ASSEMBLING QUILT

Lay all the blocks and sashes, in order, on a table or other flat surface. Following the Quilt Assembly diagram, sew a row of 2 blocks and three 18½" sashes. Trim the sashes even with the blocks. Repeat for the second row of blocks. Sew the rows together with the three 40½" sashing strips. Sew the flower and bow blocks into two rows and attach to the top and bottom sashes.

ADDING BORDERS

Cut five 1½" strips, selvage to selvage, for Border 1 and splice them as needed to make the lengths given in the Cutting Instructions. Sew the two longest strips to the sides of the quilt and trim off any extra length even with the quilt edges. Then sew the remaining strips to the top and bottom and trim as before. Repeat these steps to add Border 2.

FINISHING

Use the quick-turn method for layering the quilt and finishing the edges, then quilt as desired. Or, you can quilt the layers and finish the raw edges with binding.

QUILTING IDEAS

1. See the photo for quilting designs in the patterns.
2. Outline quilt the flowers, sashes, and inner border.
3. A 1½"–1¾" border quilting design can be used in the sashes and a 2½" – 2¾" design in the border.

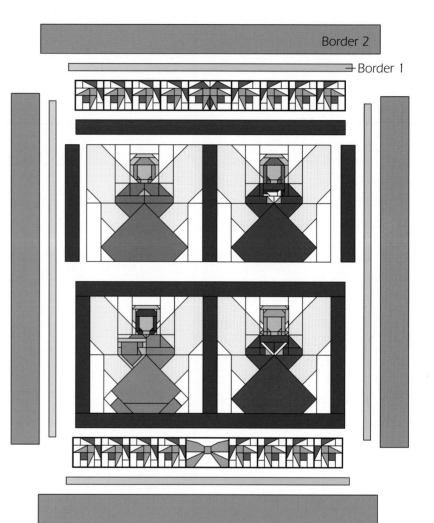

Quilt Assembly

Need Help?	
Butted corners	p. 13
Chain piecing	p. 10
Quick-turn finishing	p. 15
Rotary cutting	p. 8
Templates	p. 8

ANGEL 1

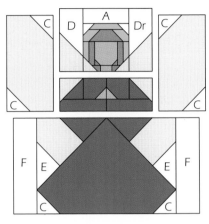

Angel 1 Assembly

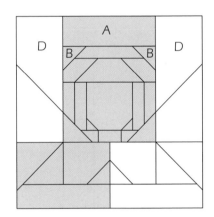

Block Sections

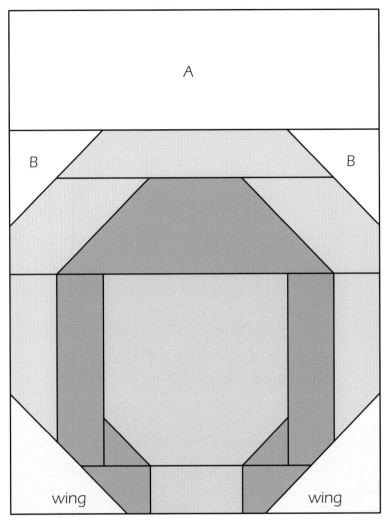

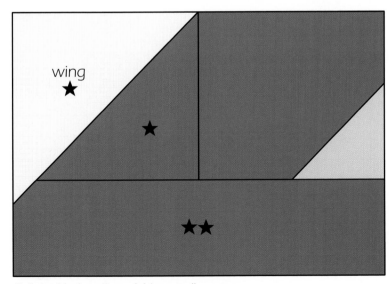

BACKGROUND ROTARY PATCHES

(for all 4 angels)

A   1¾" x 4½"

B   1⅞" x 1⅞" (h.s.)

C   2⅞" x 2⅞" (h.s.)

E   5¼" x 5¼" (q.s.)

F   2½" x 8½"

h.s. = half-square triangles
q.s. = quarter-square triangles

Full-size block sections. Add seam allowances.
★Use these patterns for Angels 2 & 3 also.
★★Use reverse for arm of Angel 3.

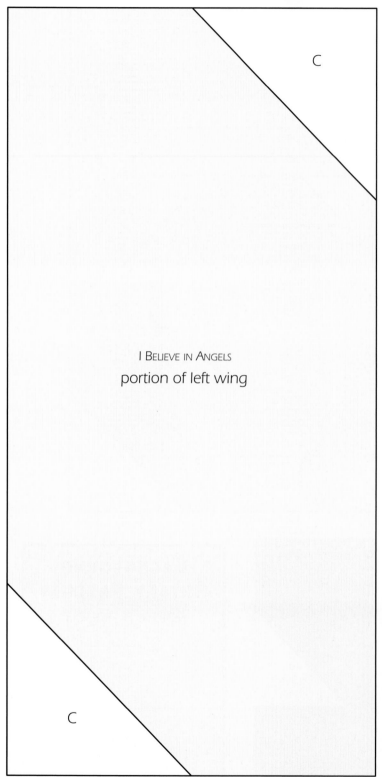

C

I BELIEVE IN ANGELS
portion of left wing

C

Full-size block sections. Reverse for right wing. Add seam allowances.
Use for all angel blocks.

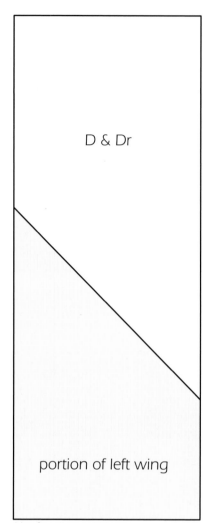

C

D & Dr

portion of left wing

Use for all angel blocks.

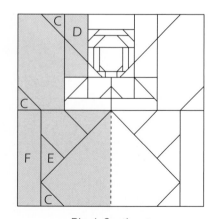

Block Sections

STITCH A CHILD'S QUILT, Vicki M. A. Thomas

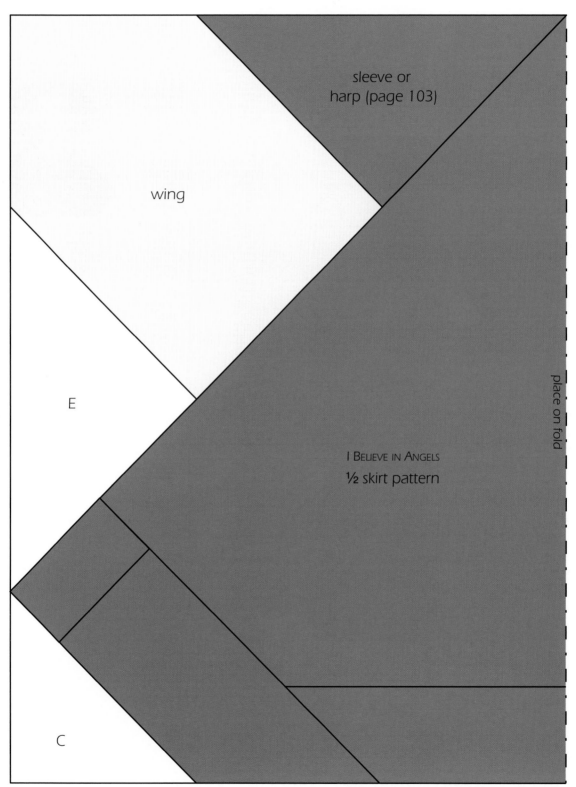

wing

sleeve or
harp (page 103)

E

I BELIEVE IN ANGELS
½ skirt pattern

place on fold

C

Full-size block section. Add seam allowances.

ANGEL 2

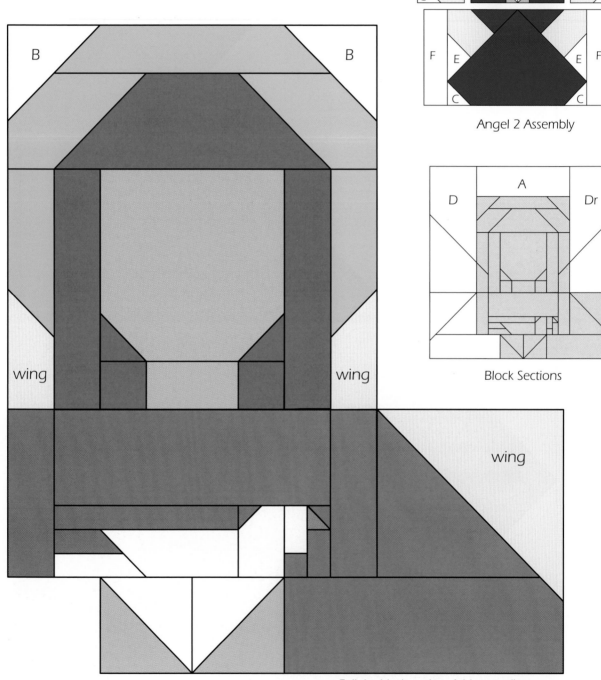

Angel 2 Assembly

Block Sections

Full-size block section. Add seam allowances.

ANGEL 3

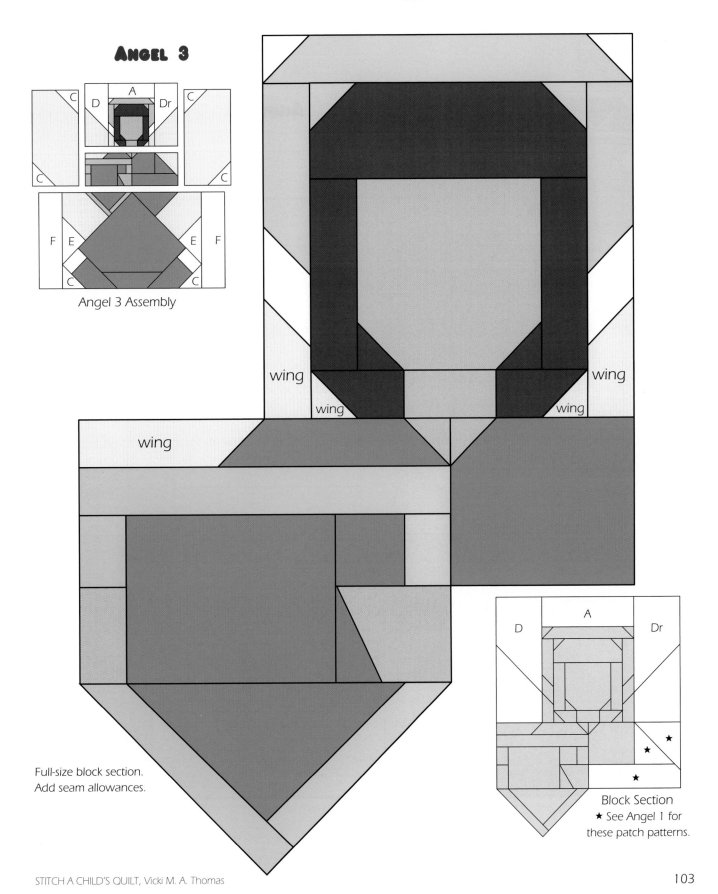

Angel 3 Assembly

wing

wing

wing

wing

wing

wing

Full-size block section.
Add seam allowances.

Block Section
★ See Angel 1 for
these patch patterns.

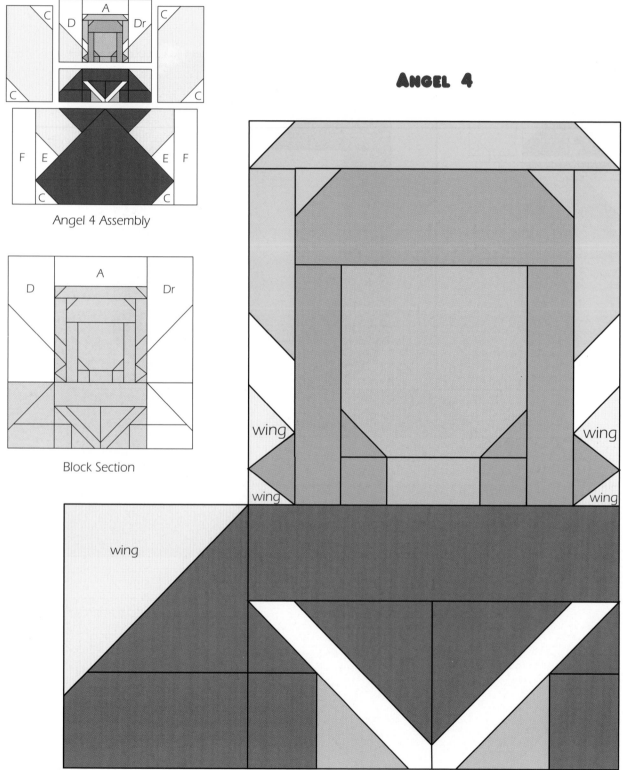

Angel 4 Assembly

Block Section

ANGEL 4

Full-size block section. Add seam allowances.

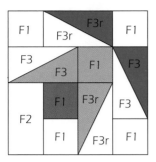

Flower Assembly

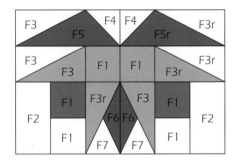

Double-Flower Assembly

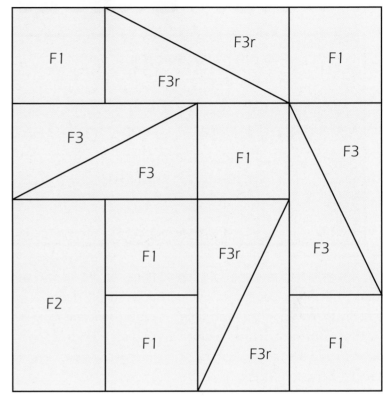

Full-size block sections. Add seam allowances.

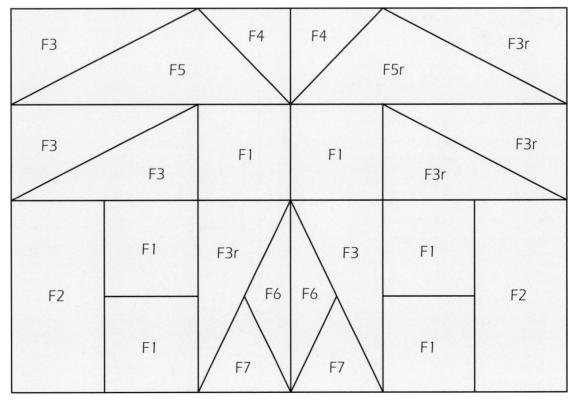

Full-size block section. Add seam allowances.

Quilt Labels for You

Supplies

Colored permanent fabric pens

Freezer paper

iron and ironing board

Light source: use a sunny window, place a small lamp
      under a plastic or glass table top or purchase a light table.

Fabric for label: muslin or light-colored fabric

A quilt label is a record of your work. It provides permanent information that will go through time with your quilt. It creates a small window into the past or, perhaps, a special occasion. It can give the recipient a note of love and fond memories.

The type and amount of information you put on a label is really a matter of personal preference, but here are some things you may want to include: the quilter's name, recipient's name, the date the quilt was finished, the occasion, a poem, words of sentiment or encouragement, and anything else of value.

Labels can take many forms. A simple piece of muslin will do just fine. You can also use pre-printed labels or a copy of a block from the front of the quilt, or you can draw your own label designs. Plain to fancy, the choice is yours.

For children's quilts, you can get ideas from coloring books, magazines, comic books, and the child's drawings. Other good designs can be found in clip art.

Books of clip art can be purchased at art-supply stores, or you can buy clip-art software for your computer. Clip-art designs are free on the internet, if you have access to it. These sources are also good places to find lettering styles.

The labels presented here are for you to use on your quilts. Whatever design you choose, start with the words. Use a ruler to draw guidelines across a piece of paper. Draw or trace the letters needed on the guidelines. Work on the paper copy until the words look the way you want them. If you have access to a computer, you can use it to work out the letter style and placement. Then print the information on paper, ready for tracing.

If you need a different size label than the ones given, you can use the following method: Design elements can be reduced or enlarged on a photocopier. Or simply change the length of the connecting lines to

create the size and shape needed. Then place either solid white paper or tracing paper on top of your words and copy them. Place this paper over the label design and copy the design elements where you want them around your words. Reposition the paper as needed. Use a ruler to draw any straight lines on your label.

When you are happy with the way it looks on paper, it is ready to be transferred to fabric. To prepare the fabric, first wash and dry it, then iron it to the shiny side of a piece of freezer paper. The freezer paper stabilizes the fabric, making it easier to write on.

For tracing, you will need a light source, either a window, a light under a plastic or glass table, or a purchased light table. Tape the design to the window or table and tape the prepared fabric over the design. Use a pencil to lightly trace the label on the fabric.

After the design and lettering have been transferred to the fabric, you can embroider the label or use fabric pens to draw over the pencil lines. Use a light touch when work-ing with pens. Fabric pens come in a variety of colors, so you can create quite beautiful designs with them. Note: Before using any pen, pre-test it on a scrap of the same fabric as your label, then wash the scrap. The ink should not bleed or wash off, and the colors should remain bright. Allow the ink to dry well. Trim off excess fabric, leaving enough for a turn-under allowance all around the label, and peel the freezer paper from the fabric. Use a small appliqué stitch to sew the label to the quilt backing.

MORE QUILT LABELS

GLOSSARY

Appliqué: A design cut from several pieces of fabric and stitched to a plain piece of fabric. Usually the design pieces are hand sewn with the blind-hem or blanket stitch.

Assembly-line piecing: (also called chain piecing) In this sewing technique, patches are cut and set out in sewing order alongside your machine. The patches are sewn together one after the other without removing them from the machine. They can then be ironed before being cut apart.

Backing: The fabric used to make the back of the quilt. It can be made from one solid piece or from pieces stitched together. The backing is normally made 4" longer and wider than the quilt top.

Backstitch: (also called back-tacking) Sewing in reverse for a few stitches to anchor the thread instead of making a knot.

Basting: Running stitches used to hold the layers together for quilting. These stitches are not permanent and will be removed after quilting. Basting may also be done using safety pins instead of thread.

Batting: The fiber filler between the quilt top and the back. The batting is what gives the quilt its thickness and warmth.

Bias: Diagonal to the grain of the weave. The bias of fabric has more elasticity than the lengthwise or crosswise grain. Bias strips can be used for binding quilts.

Binding: The edge finishing for a quilt. It is made of a straight-grain or bias strip of fabric sewn to cover the raw edges of a quilt.

Block: A design unit in a quilt top. A block is usually square, but it may be a triangle, rectangle, hexagon, or any shape that, when repeated, makes the complete quilt top design.

Blocking: The use of a steam iron to press the quilt blocks and ensure that they are flat and square. Some gentle coaxing into shape may be required.

Border: A frame for the quilt blocks. Quilts can have single or multiple borders or no border at all. Many borders are pieced or appliquéd.

Chain piece: To sew pattern pieces together one after the other without lifting the presser foot or removing them from the machine. The small chains of thread between the sewn pieces are cut after sewing many or all of the pieces.

Echo quilting: (also called outline quilting) Multiple quilting lines, placed at equal intervals, used to outline a patch.

Grain: The horizontal or vertical direction of the threads in the fabric weave.

Grid: To quilt a pattern in evenly spaced horizontal, vertical, or diagonal lines forming squares or diamonds across an area of the quilt top. Grids are used as background patterns or fillers.

Hand quilting: The process of sewing all three layers of a quilt together by hand, generally by using a short running stitch.

Label: To mark your finished quilt with your name, the date the quilt was made, and any comments you wish to make. Labels are frequently made by writing on fabric, usually muslin, with indelible ink or stitching. Labels are generally attached to the back of the quilt. Historians use labels to help them identify and date quilts.

Layering: Assembling the quilt top, batting, and backing. The layers are basted with thread or safety pins to keep them from shifting as they are being quilted.

Machine quilting: The process of stitching through all the quilt layers with a sewing machine to create a quilted design.

Marking: Drawing the desired quilting pattern on the quilt top by using a removable marker, removable pencil, or masking tape. This may be done freehand or with stencils.

Miter: Joining two strips together to form a 45-degree angled seam. Borders and bindings frequently have mitered corners.

Nine patch: A block made of nine smaller patches or blocks arranged in three rows of three.

Quilting: The stitching that creates a design on the quilt top and back, while holding the three layers of the quilt together. Quilting may be done by hand or machine.

Quilting in the ditch: Quilting stitches done in the seam lines.

Running stitch: A line of short, even stitches used in hand quilting.

Sashing: (also called lattice strips) Small strips of fabric located between the the quilt blocks.

Seam allowance: The distance between the seam line and the cutting line of a pattern piece. For quilting, the standard width is ¼".

Self-binding: Folding the quilt backing around to the front of the quilt to form the quilt binding.

Selvages: The finished edges on fabric yardage. Selvages are discarded when cutting fabric pieces because the tighter weave can create problems in stitching and shrinks relative to the regular fabric weave.

Stencil: A plastic, metal, or paper guide used to draw a quilting pattern or design on the quilt top.

Template: A reusable plastic, cardboard, or sturdy paper pattern used as a guide for marking on fabric. Templates are used for cutting patches, appliqué, and for marking quilting patterns.

AQS Books on Quilts

This is only a partial listing of the books available from the American Quilter's Society. AQS books are known worldwide for timely topics, clear writing, beautiful color photos, and accurate illustrations and patterns. The following books are available from your local bookseller, quilt shop, or public library. If you are unable to locate certain titles in your area, you may order by mail from the AMERICAN QUILTER'S SOCIETY, P.O. Box 3290, Paducah, KY 42002-3290. Add $2.00 for postage for the first book ordered and 40¢ for each additional book. Include item number, title, and price when ordering. Allow 14 to 21 days for delivery. Customers with Visa, MasterCard, or Discover may phone in orders from 7:00–5:00 CST, Mon.–Fri., 1-800-626-5420.

4595	**Above & Beyond Basics**, Karen Kay Buckley	$18.95
4813	**Addresses & Birthdays**, compiled by Klaudeen Hansen **(HB)**	$14.95
4543	**American Quilt Blocks: 50 Patterns for 50 States**, Beth Summers	$16.95
4696	**Amish Kinder Komforts**, Bettina Havig	$14.95
4829	**Anita Shackelford: Surface Textures**, Anita Shackelford **(HB)**	$24.95
4899	**Appliqué Paper Greetings**, Elly Sienkiewicz **(HB)**	$24.95
3790	**Appliqué Patterns from Native American Beadwork Designs**, Dr. Joyce Mori	$14.95
5234	**Appliqué with Folded Cutwork**, Anita Shackelford	$22.95
2099	**Ask Helen: More About Quilting Designs**, Helen Squire	$14.95
2207	**Award-Winning Quilts: 1985–1987**	$24.95
2354	**Award-Winning Quilts: 1988–1989**	$24.95
3425	**Award-Winning Quilts: 1990–1991**	$24.95
3791	**Award-Winning Quilts: 1992–1993**	$24.95
4830	**Baskets: Celtic Style**, Scarlett Rose	$19.95
4832	**A Batch of Patchwork**, May T. Miller & Susan B. Burton	$18.95
5175	**Blooms & Baskets**, Emily G. Senuta	$24.95
4593	**Blossoms by the Sea: Making Ribbon Flowers for Quilts**, Faye Labanaris	$24.95
4898	**Borders & Finishing Touches**, Bonnie K. Browning	$16.95
4957	**Carrie Hall Blocks**, Bettina Havig	$34.95
4697	**Caryl Bryer Fallert: A Spectrum of Quilts**, 1983-1995, Caryl Bryer Fallert	$24.95
4626	**Celtic Geometric Quilts**, Camille Remme	$16.95
3926	**Celtic Style Floral Appliqué**, Scarlett Rose	$14.95
2208	**Classic Basket Quilts**, Elizabeth Porter & Marianne Fons	$16.95
5235	**Create with Helen Squire: Hand & Machine Quilting**, Helen Squire	$18.95
4827	**Dating Fabrics: A Color Guide 1800–1960**, Eileen Jahnke Trestain	$24.95
4818	**Dear Helen, Can You Tell Me?** Helen Squire	$15.95
3399	**Dye Painting!** Ann Johnston	$19.95
4814	**Encyclopedia of Designs for Quilting**, Phyllis D. Miller **(HB)**	$34.95
3468	**Encyclopedia of Pieced Quilt Patterns**, compiled by Barbara Brackman	$34.95
4594	**Firm Foundations**, Jane Hall & Dixie Haywood	$18.95
4900	**Four Blocks Continued…**, Linda Giesler Carlson	$16.95
2381	**From Basics to Binding**, Karen Kay Buckley	$16.95
4628	**Helen's Guide to quilting in the 21st century**, Helen Squire	$16.95
1906	**Irish Chain Quilts: A Workbook of Irish Chains**, Joyce B. Peaden	$14.95
5296	**Kaleidoscope: New Quilts From an Old Favorite**	$16.95
4751	**Liberated Quiltmaking**, Gwen Marston **(HB)**	$24.95
4897	**Lois Smith's Machine Quiltmaking**, Lois Smith	$19.95
4545	**Log Cabin with a Twist**, Barbara T. Kaempfer	$18.95
4815	*Love to Quilt:* **Bears, Bears, Bears**, Karen Kay Buckley	$14.95
4833	*Love to Quilt:* **Broderie Perse: The Elegant Quilt**, Barbara W. Barber	$14.95
4890	*Love to Quilt:* **Dye & Discharge, Playing on Fabric**, Sara Newberg King	$14.95
4816	*Love to Quilt:* **Necktie Sampler Blocks**, Janet B. Elwin	$14.95
4753	*Love to Quilt:* **Penny Squares**, Willa Baranowski	$12.95
5013	*Love to Quilt:* **Petal by Petal**, Joan Shay	$14.95
4995	**Magic Stack-n-Whack Quilts™**, Bethany S. Reynolds	$19.95
4911	**Mariner's Compass Quilts: New Quilts from an Old Favorite**	$16.95
4752	**Miniature Quilts: Connecting New & Old Worlds**, Tina M. Gravatt	$14.95
3871	**Museum of the American Quilter's Society**	$6.95
1981	**Nancy Crow: Quilts and Influences**, Nancy Crow **(HB)**	$29.95
3331	**Nancy Crow: Work in Transition**, Nancy Crow	$12.95
5177	**Native American Designs for Quilting**, Dr. Joyce Mori	$15.95
4828	**Nature, Design & Silk Ribbons**, Cathy Grafton	$18.95
4889	**Navigating Compass Designs**, Barbara Ann Caron	$19.95
3332	**New Jersey Quilts**, The Heritage Quilt Project of New Jersey	$29.95
3927	**New Patterns from Old Architecture**, Carol Wagner	$12.95
4627	**Ohio Star Quilts: New Quilts from an Old Favorite**	$16.95
5210	**One Block = Many Quilts**, Agnete Kay	$18.95
4831	**Optical Illusions for Quilters**, Karen Combs	$22.95
4515	**Paint and Patches: Painting on Fabrics with Pigment**, Vicki L. Johnson	$18.95
5434	**Paper Piecing Patterns**, Bonnie K. Browning	$14.95
5098	**Pineapple Quilts: New Quilts from an Old Favorite**	$16.95
4779	**Protecting Your Quilts: A Guide for Quilt Owners, Second Edition**	$6.95
5200	**Quilt Art Engagement Calendar**	$9.95
2380	**Quilter's Registry**, Lynne Fritz	$9.95
3467	**Quilting Patterns from Native American Designs**, Dr. Joyce Mori	$12.95
3470	**Quilting with Style**, Gwen Marston & Joe Cunningham	$24.95
2284	**Quiltmaker's Guide: Basics & Beyond**, Carol Doak	$19.95
4918	**Quilts by Paul D. Pilgrim: Blending the Old & the New**, Gerald E. Roy	$16.95
2257	*Quilts:* **The Permanent Collection – MAQS**	$9.95
3793	*Quilts:* **The Permanent Collection – MAQS Volume II**	$9.95
5106	**Quilts with a View**, Faye Labanaris	$16.95
5140	**Ribbons & Threads: Baltimore Style**, Bonnie K. Browning	$14.95
3789	**Roots, Feathers & Blooms**, Linda Giesler Carlson	$16.95
5176	**Sew Many Stars**, Gail Searl	$22.95
4783	**Silk Ribbons by Machine**, Jeanie Sexton	$15.95
5298	**Show Me Helen: How to Use Quilting Designs**, Helen Squire	$16.95
5236	**Stitch a Child's Quilt**, Vicki M. A. Thomas	$18.95
3929	**The Stori Book of Embellishing**, Mary Stori	$16.95
5211	**String Quilts with Style**, Bobbie Aug & Sharon Newman	$18.95
5012	**Take-Away Appliqué**, Suzanne Marshall	$22.95
3930	**Tessellations & Variations**, Barbara Ann Caron	$14.95
3788	**Three-Dimensional Appliqué**, Anita Shackelford	$24.95
4596	**Ties, Ties, Ties: Traditional Quilts from Neckties**, Janet B. Elwin	$19.95
3931	**Time-Span Quilts: New Quilts from Old Tops**, Becky Herdle	$16.95
4919	**Transforming Fabric**, Carolyn Dahl **(HB)**	$29.95
5297	**Treasury of Crazyquilt Stitches**, Carole Samples	$26.95
2029	**A Treasury of Quilting Designs**, Linda Goodmon Emery	$14.95
4956	**Variegreat! New Dimensions in Traditional Quilts**, Linda Glantz	$19.95
5014	**The Wholecloth Garment Stori**, Mary Stori	$19.95
5237	**2000 Wall Calendar**	$8.95
2286	**Wonderful Wearables: A Celebration of Creative Clothing**, Virginia Avery	$24.95